Grit, Grime, and Glory

Stories of Hope from a World of Hard-Living People

Many blessings,
Rhonda Bandy

RHONDA WHITNEY BANDY, PHD

WESTBOW
PRESS®
A DIVISION OF THOMAS NELSON
& ZONDERVAN

WestBow Press books may be ordered through booksellers or by contacting:

WestBow Press
A Division of Thomas Nelson & Zondervan
1663 Liberty Drive
Bloomington, IN 47403
www.westbowpress.com
1 (866) 928-1240

ISBN: 978-1-9736-7464-1 (sc)
ISBN: 978-1-9736-7466-5 (hc)
ISBN: 978-1-9736-7465-8 (e)

Library of Congress Control Number: 2019914319

Print information available on the last page.

WestBow Press rev. date: 09/25/2019

CONTENTS

Part 2: PACS Moves

Part 3: God's Leading

DEDICATION

I lovingly dedicate this book to the governing board, staff, and volunteers of Portland Adventist Community Services (PACS). When I became the executive director of PACS, I determined not to become attached to those I worked with because most were much older than me, and I knew someday I would lose them. Fortunately, I was not successful in this endeavor. Despite my foolish intentions, these faithful volunteers became my dear friends and family. Unfortunately, my initial fears became reality, but my life has been exponentially enriched by the wisdom and unlimited love each one role-modeled and imprinted on me. I would have it no other way. Those I have lost and those who remain will always be part of my heart. This humble, candid book is for them.

DISCLAIMER

This easy-to-read book is packed with stories. There are funny stories, sad stories, tragic stories, and everyday stories. You can find them all here. Even though you may be tempted to disbelieve some of them, these accounts are all true. I've taken the liberty to add snippets of conversation to make them sensible to you, because you couldn't be there in person. I've tried to verify the accuracy of the first-person accounts. All names have been changed unless otherwise specified, and sometimes details have been removed or altered to protect the privacy of individuals.

These stories reflect either my own experiences or as I remember them being told to me. I take full credit for anything I may have omitted or inaccurately presented.

PREFACE

To understand the exciting stories you are about to read, you will need some detailed background. I'll try to help you picture the context of the physical place and the working culture in which these sometimes unbelievable experiences occurred.

Portland Adventist Community Services (PACS) is a relief agency providing food, health care, clothing, and household items to low-income people. It is supported by nine Seventh-day Adventist churches in the Portland, Oregon, area. PACS is widely respected by governmental and faith-based sectors alike; it is considered a major part of the social service infrastructure of Portland, Oregon.

When I came to the agency in 1994, it was relatively small, had a cash budget of $25,000 per year, and served approximately 18,000 people each year with free food, clothing, and medical care. Though lacking any formal fundraising, business structure, or volunteer program, the services were offered consistently every morning, four mornings a week. The health clinic had already been established in 1993 by the previous executive director, Barbara Nelson (real name); Walla Walla University School of Nursing; and Portland Adventist Medical Center. The program continued to expand. The staff and governing board resolved to provide service with more dignity, so the free clothing program was changed to a thrift store ministry in 1996.

Due to overcrowding and a giant increase in demand for services, we moved the agency in 1998. The original old, dark building was a dilapidated, three-storied, handicap-inaccessible, 12,000-square-foot building with only five parking spaces for clients. It had served its purpose well over the years, but now it was not adequate. The new building, an old supermarket turned athletic fitness center, was twice as large; was more accessible to cars, public busses, and foot traffic; and allowed for continued advances in program delivery. This facility was all on one level, was completely renovated with tasteful decorations, was newly painted in subtle mauves and greens, and had nearly fifty parking spaces.

Because of the transition and a wish to add freedom of choice to the principle of providing dignity, the food box program was transformed to a grocery store–style food pantry where people could choose their own food from the shelves according to the needs of their families.

God blessed abundantly, and when I left PACS in 2007, the budget was approximately $3.5 million, which included both cash and donated goods. The agency had a small paid staff and more than 200 volunteers. We served over 250,000 individuals each year with food, clothing, and household articles through the thrift and food ministries, including approximately 1,100 patients being treated at the clinic each year.

Understanding the Book Title

Grit, Grime, and Glory describes the everyday atmosphere of PACS. Working in social service agencies often takes guts and perseverance. The work is hard and often filthy. Yet during it all, God chooses to show up in marvelous ways, turning the difficult and mundane into unexpected, unmistakable bursts of glory.

The term "hard-living people," as referenced in this book, refers to two different groups of individuals. "Hard living" is a term I first encountered when reading the excellent book *Hard Living People and Mainstream Christians* (1993) by Tex Sample. Like Sample, I use "hard-living people" to describe the people we served because life was often hard for them, and they lived it valiantly. Unlike Sample, I also use "hard living" to describe the volunteers and others who worked tirelessly, hour after hour, to minister to their neighbors.

Hard-living people are often misunderstood. We have stereotypical opinions of people who we think are working the system, who make what seem to us to be poor choices, who get caught in the downward spiral of poverty, who we think lack smarts, or even who use violence to get what they want. Sometimes those opinions are true, but most of the time they are not.

Those stereotypical opinions are sometimes extended to those who step out to lend a helping hand. They are often accused of being enablers, being easily duped, and encouraging people to be lazy. You can't do this work and not be misunderstood by someone, somewhere, sometime.

ACKNOWLEDGMENTS

Though it is my honor to document these experiences, I wish to give credit and thanks to the clients and volunteers at PACS, and especially to the Lord Jesus, who made it all possible. The list of those who contributed in various ways to the making of this book is long. If I tried to name everyone, someone would most certainly be left out. If you've ever had anything to do with PACS and think your name should appear here, you are right. It takes a village to create a book of this kind.

I also wish to thank my husband, Owen Bandy, for his patience through the hours of writing and his willingness to read every story, asking questions until he understood each one. His support gave me the resolve to continue writing when myriads of other things clamored for my attention.

In addition, I wish to thank those along the way who have encouraged me and provided capable, editorial direction in moving these stories from rough draft to finished manuscript. Their help and encouragement were invaluable.

Lastly, if you choose to share any of these stories with others, please remember to give God the glory. Without the Lord, this book would not exist. May these stories inspire you as you embark on the story of Jesus interacting with His children in a tiny corner of Portland, Oregon, in these United States of America.

INTRODUCTION

O ver the years, many people urged me to write a book about my experience at PACS, so I have written what I remember. In these pages, you will find stories of miracles, struggles, despair, and generosity. Each one describes a place where the forces of evil clashed with the might of God.

These experiences fit within the framework of a larger story of an organization growing, thriving, contracting, and undulating from 1994 to 2007. These were years of tumultuous social, political, and economic upheaval. The events happened during a time when the federal government changed welfare laws, hoping to reduce government spending. This strategy may have worked for Uncle Sam, but many people lost their homes, hunger became rampant, and medical care grew too expensive to use. An event memorialized in history as 9/11 slammed the country, forever changing life for everyone as they rushed to give up personal and corporate freedoms. Terrorism was officially on American soil. It no longer felt safe to move freely in the United States.

Along with 9/11 came a national economic crunch, intensifying this perfect storm of catastrophes. Businesses closed. Many Americans found themselves in financial crisis. At the same time, both legal and illegal immigration was strong, creating even longer lines for emergency food, clothing, and medical care.

Jobs evaporated. Charitable giving plummeted. Yet despite the challenges, PACS continued to serve and thrive.

This is also the story of an amazing group of volunteers giving, caring, flexing, loving, and praying through topsy-turvy years of growth, relocation, and demands from all sides. This is the story of faithful governing board members who patiently steered this little organization through a crazy time to become a large agency. Community partners played key roles in providing support and relief. The Oregon Food Bank, Trader Joe's, Portland Adventist Medical Center, the Oregon Conference of Seventh-day Adventists, Walla Walla University School of Nursing, the Multnomah County Health Department, along with foundations, churches, schools, and individual donors, were among the scores of contributors committed to PACS and to their communities.

I couldn't have known all this when I applied for the mildly intriguing job of executive director of PACS. *Community services?* I naively thought when I was offered the position. *How hard can it be?* Unbeknownst to me, I was about to embark on the most difficult and exhilarating years of my life.

PART ONE

Mistakes, Surprises, and Blessings

Fledgling Years of Servanthood

1

CHAPTER

Smelly Old Clothes

My history with social services agencies was almost nil before I became executive director at Portland Adventist Community Services (PACS). I had heard of PACS through some friends, so I knew the agency was run by volunteers and that it gave out food and clothing. The church I attended in my childhood had a ministry called Dorcas, based on the Bible story of a woman named Dorcas who sewed clothes for the poor. The church Dorcas of my childhood also helped the poor, and my childish perception was that it was run by old women wearing what I called "grandma shoes." The black, lace-up shoes had small, cut-out designs in the leather uppers. They were supported by sturdy, black soles and thick, two-inch-high, clunky heels. I thought PACS might be like my memories of Dorcas.

I had never visited PACS before getting a job there, so I had a lot to learn. Neither had I ever been a recipient of charity, except for one time as a child. One of my earliest memories was going to a Christmas party in January, given by the Red Cross for the children of my hometown.

On Christmas Eve that year, our town had been ravished by a flood. Without warning, a levee broke, and a wall of water from the nearby river raged through the town. Sounding like a freight train, it overtook fleeing residents and drowned farm animals. In the havoc, most people lost everything. Some lost their lives.

Christmas was literally washed away in our town. Because of the trauma and loss endured by the community, the Red Cross decided to throw a late Christmas party to bring some cheer to children and their suffering families by distributing presents.

I remember meeting Santa Claus for the first time. I observed him solemnly, staring unblinkingly as only a newly turned three-year-old can do. Everyone from the small town was crowded into the Odd Fellow's Hall. The mood was jovial, and Santa was in fine form, distributing toys to every boy and girl. My toy turned out to be a small, stuffed plastic elephant trimmed in red blanket stitching, with tiny red flowers printed all over its stark white body. My disappointment was immediate because the seams were scratchy and the elephant was cold, even though it was a bit squishy. I wanted something soft and cuddly. Even so, something drew me to that cold little elephant. The trunk was handy to grab, which resulted over the years in cracking off all the plastic. When I became a sophomore in college, I finally gave him up. But I knew that when living was hard, it meant a lot that someone cared.

My limited exposure to poverty was a skimpy starting point for working at PACS. It hardly prepared me for the huge learning curve I would experience and the intimate knowledge I would gain over the years. In addition, I was not prepared for the experiences of what some might call serendipitous happenings or luck but what I accepted as providence of God.

The volunteers loved to tell me of the amazing things that had happened before I came on the scene. Their faces shone as they eagerly recounted to me, the newbie in the building, about various wonderful remembrances from the past. One happened not long before I joined the PACS family.

Money was an ongoing need at PACS: money to buy food to distribute, money to put gas in the trucks that collected food from local grocery stores, money for the phone bill, money for the heat bill, money for supplies, money for garbage service, money for more things than one could imagine. This was a common problem brought to the Lord in morning worship. It was part of prayer time nearly every day.

This time at morning worship, they needed money to pay for utilities. One payment had already been missed, and now they must pay both the current month and the previous month, which totaled $1,200. They reminded the Lord they couldn't help people if the lights, heat, and water were shut off because the bills hadn't been paid. They expectantly asked Him to stretch out His arms and help them in their dire predicament. They finished by confidently thanking Him for supplying their need. Then, like they did every day after telling the Lord about their difficulties and making their petitions, they got up off their knees and matter-of-factly went to work. A busy day of boxing up food and sorting clothes loomed ahead. They were confident an answer would come and left it up to the Lord because they trusted Him.

Down in the basement where donations were sorted, a bunch of old clothes had recently been dropped off. No one knew where they came from, but it was just as well because the clothes were old and mostly threadbare. Helga, the assistant director, was tempted to throw them all out but decided to at least look them over. She'd had plenty of experience doing this and went deftly through everything, checking for missing buttons and stuff left in the pockets.

One of the items was an old, deep-burgundy, velour bathrobe. She held it up; it was clearly loved and worn. It was too old to be given away, so she quickly checked the pockets. Suddenly, she felt a lump. *Probably a tissue,* she thought.

After thrusting her hand deep into the pocket, she grabbed a wad of something. She pulled it out to investigate. No, it was not a tissue. *What was it?* It looked like old, dirty paper held together with deteriorating rubber bands. She opened it curiously and then realized it was money. Helga thought it might be a couple hundred dollars—an exorbitant amount to find in an old, abandoned pocket.

A trained accountant with experience in ethically handling money, Helga didn't unfold the bills by herself. She rushed to the director's office, and they counted it together. It was exactly $1,200—just what they had asked for that morning in worship.

Not only was there great rejoicing and immediate thanks given to God, but this story was still being told by joyous volunteers when I came to PACS. I wondered whether anything would ever happen like that while I was there.

2

Refrigerator Needed

The week I became director at PACS, I tried to learn what was happening in the agency. First, I visited the clothing department on the main level of the building. The next day, I went to the basement and visited the food department, where there was an odd assortment of commercial and home-style refrigerators and freezers. In the kitchen, I found volunteers scurrying about their daily duties. I asked how I could help, hoping to learn the systems and how everything worked. The volunteers politely, firmly, and succinctly told me my job was to be the director, and I should go back to my office and take care of director-type matters. I dutifully retreated to my office upstairs; the volunteer crew changed daily, so I resolved to visit them later. This plan was successful, and I soon learned the kitchen system.

The next day, I stayed upstairs where my office was located and went directly across the hall to visit the PACS Family Health Clinic. It was busy also, although with a more subdued, antiseptic atmosphere that was appropriate and professional. The clinic, comprised of three exam rooms, was located on one side of a big conference room, so it didn't take long to grasp the flow and determine the equipment on hand.

As I looked around, I discovered there was no refrigerator. I knew many medicines and lab tests must be kept cold—and in those days, they could be kept in the same refrigerator—so I asked, "How are you managing without a refrigerator? Where are you putting labs and medicines that need to be kept cold?"

"Oh, we use a shelf of the refrigerator in the staff kitchen. It's on the other side of the conference room," they answered.

Legally, medicines and lab samples could not be kept in a refrigerator with food. I knew we needed a designated refrigerator for labs and medicines. At the same time, I had seen the latest financial report and knew we didn't have the money to buy a new refrigerator. I pondered how to get the equipment necessary for a well-run clinic.

Suddenly, a perfectly logical thought popped into my mind. Impulsively, I picked up the phone and called my church. "Can I put an advertisement in our church bulletin?" I asked.

"Sure," was the reply. In no time, we drafted a three-line request for a refrigerator for PACS.

Not too many people have extra refrigerators, so I'm not sure it will do any good, but at least we can ask, I thought.

A few days later, I went to church. I'd forgotten about the ad. Just before the sermon, someone behind me tapped my shoulder and said, "Do you need a refrigerator?"

Puzzled for a moment, I wondered what they were talking about. Then I remembered the ad. "Yes, I do," I replied.

"Well, I've got one that is almost brand-new, and I'd be happy to donate that." I was excited. Wow! God had answered so quickly and easily. This was fun!

Then on the way out of church, another person stopped me and said, "I see you need a refrigerator."

I didn't know what to say. I didn't want to say, "Oh, we already have one." So I just said, "Thank you," and let them be excited about their gift. I didn't know how to refuse them.

I went home. On Sunday morning, the phone rang. "Do you need a refrigerator?" a voice asked.

By that time, I had already accepted two refrigerators, and I couldn't tell this person no. I said, "Yes, that will be wonderful!" By the end of the day, two more people called, and I ended up accepting five refrigerators. I was amazed at the generosity of the Lord, but I was also concerned.

I slipped into work early Monday morning without being seen. I should never have accepted all those refrigerators. We only needed one, not five. At the time, we were not giving away furniture, so none of our clients would ask for a refrigerator. No refrigerators had been delivered yet, so no one knew of my blunder.

At worship that morning, I sheepishly confessed to the volunteers what I had done. I apologized profusely, promising to get the appliances removed from the agency as quickly as possible. Their response caught me by surprise. Instead of complaining, they said, "Praise the Lord! I wonder what He's going to do with them?" That attitude was a new concept to me.

At about 10:30 a.m., my phone rang. The Immigrant and Refugee Community Organization (IRCO) had never called before, but they needed a refrigerator. *Great,* I thought. *That's one refrigerator down.*

The voice said, "We need a refrigerator because we have some families coming in on the plane from Russia. They're coming in at 1:00 p.m., and we have apartments ready for all of them, but we don't have a refrigerator."

I noted he mentioned "families" and "apartments," so I asked, "How many refrigerators do you need?"

"We're furnishing four apartments, and each apartment needs a refrigerator," he explained.

"Do you have enough refrigerators?" I queried, somehow knowing the answer already.

"No, but we thought we'd start by asking if you had at least one. We still have to find the rest," he responded.

I swallowed hard. "I can give you four!" I exclaimed.

I couldn't believe the incredible way God had answered my simple request for just one refrigerator. With one small church bulletin advertisement, not only did He take care of our need, but He also met the needs of four families flying in from Russia that very week.

My faith began to grow.

3

Twenty-Four Hours with God

Things were rough. It seemed we always struggled to find enough money. Most of our equipment was inadequate, obsolete, or worn. For example, our small copier quit altogether. The truck we used every day to pick up food and household donations was battered, had extremely high mileage, and needed major repairs.

Our method for answering phones was embarrassingly antiquated. One phone rang in the basement. When the call was for someone on the main floor or the second floor of the building, the receptionist hollered up the stairwell, screaming for whomever she needed. She was good at her job. She barked like a drill sergeant in a voice that could be heard clearly in every corner of the agency. It was effective but not very businesslike.

We had other challenges as well, such as not enough space and barely enough money to cover our utilities, much less to buy food and other necessities for our clients. We faithfully brought these needs to the Lord every morning.

One day in a planning meeting, the volunteers requested a time of fasting and prayer outside of work hours, to have a longer time to fully focus on our prayer time with the Lord. We carefully made plans and prepared our hearts. We started Friday evening with foot washing, partaking of the Lord's Supper, and celebrating communion (or Eucharist, as some churches call it). Then we talked to the Lord, and on a big flip chart, we made a list of our requests to Him.

I wrote each request as the volunteers suggested it. They mentioned many things, both for the agency and for personal needs, such as health or family. Some things were simple; others were more serious. Suddenly, one volunteer, a tiny little lady, offered simply, "Let's pray for a new copy machine." I gulped. I knew we needed it, but copy machines were expensive. I wrote it down.

Then another volunteer said, "Let's pray for a new truck." I gulped again. How would God answer these requests? These volunteers were so trusting, so believing. Inwardly I apologized to God for their boldness, but I wrote it down just like I had listed the copier.

Finally, the last person said, "Let's pray for a new phone system." I knew there was no way we would get a phone system. Much as we needed it, the building was old, we had no money, and companies didn't give away phone systems. I wrote it down, but I cringed to think how I would explain it when the childlike faith of these volunteers was not honored.

We started praying. Throughout the night, there was always a group of two or more, awake and praying. We all met together the next morning. As we went from room to room, we prayed for the ministry and the volunteers who performed each ministry. We prayed fervently for each other. Tears often fell amidst assurances of love and Christian concern. We finished with sundown worship and a light meal. No one knew of our prayer list.

We experienced a precious spiritual high together. I sensed a greater unity than I'd ever sensed before.

On Monday, the mundane returned; it was business as usual. On Tuesday morning, my phone rang. It was a friend. "Do you guys need a new truck?" he said. "We've figured out how to get one for you."

I put down the phone in awe. *A new truck? That's unreal! That only happens in stories, not in real life.*

We thanked the Lord, and I was happy. Maybe this would alleviate the disappointment of the volunteers when the other two major requests were not answered.

On Wednesday, the phone rang again. "Many months ago, we placed a demonstration copier in your agency," a voice said. I remembered. We had been going from company to company, asking for demonstration machines for the last year. That was the only way we'd been able to get by when the old one quit. The machine this person was talking about was the first machine we had tried out, and it was our favorite. It cost $25,000 and did everything we wanted, but we couldn't afford it.

"Another company bought a machine exactly like the one you tried," the salesman continued. "It wasn't big enough for them, so after using it for two weeks, they returned it. We can let you have it for $9,000 because it is now used." Dazed, I passed the word along to the volunteers. Our fundraiser got on the phone, called several donors, and raised the money in just two hours.

I started telling everyone about how God had answered our prayers. I didn't care whether He hadn't answered them all; I was simply thrilled with what He gave us. My faith soared.

On Friday, the phone rang. "Hi there," a familiar voice greeted me. After a little small talk, he came to the point. "I'm going into business and am wondering whether I could use your agency as a demonstration."

"Sure, but what kind of business?" I was puzzled.

"I'm working for a phone company, and I need to install a system to show my customers how great it is. It's worth $14,000, but I will give it to you for free."

What? Really? Wow! All three of the "impossible" requests had been answered within a week. I was dumbfounded and couldn't quit praising God for this demonstration of His willingness to give good gifts to His children, as Jesus promised in Matthew 7:11.

I never forgot those simple, heartfelt requests from volunteers whose faith seemed presumptuous to me. I saw my faith as more realistic and sophisticated than theirs. The Lord answered in ways I could never have imagined. I began to realize the shallowness of my own spiritual experience. He didn't rebuke me or punish me. He lovingly showed me to expect great things from the God, Who owns it all.

4

CHAPTER

"That's Jesus!"

Outside my office on the broad, dark maroon, carpet-covered steps, I heard the pitter-patter of tiny feet going up and down, up and down, up and down. I never stayed in my office for any length of time, so when I came out to check on something else, I found the little child whose footsteps I was hearing. She was a busy little girl of about four years old. She was intent on her mission of repeatedly conquering the stairs, so she didn't see me at first. When she glanced up at me, I could tell her shoulder-length brown hair hadn't been combed for days; her eyes were underlined by dark circles, and her tiny dress was crumpled and dirty.

She was beginning to tire of the stairs while waiting for her mother to pick out clothes downstairs, and she sat down on the top step to survey the world below. Her mother could clearly see her on the stairs while the little girl watched her mother systematically sift through the clothing racks.

"Hi," I said softly.

She took her gaze from the scene below and looked up at me. She didn't answer and continued to stare unblinkingly back at me. I calmly joined her on the stairs. As I sat down beside her, I noticed bruises on her arms and face. Her sleeveless dress couldn't conceal the black and blue marks, mostly faded now, which darkened her thin arms. She drew her skirt over her bare legs. I knew this child had suffered harm; her unflinching gaze and remoteness told me she was both resigned and wary.

We sat on the stairs in silence for a few moments, absorbing the sounds of conversation drifting up from the people we could see milling about below. Our noses breathed in the smell of old clothes, and our hands felt the scratchiness of the short-pile burgundy carpet. We sat in silence, getting comfortable in each other's presence.

Finally, she began to stir. "I'm Sarah," she began.

"Hi, Sarah. I'm Rhonda," I replied. Then we made small talk about things interesting to a four-year old. While we were talking, I noticed a sticker placed on her hand by one of the interviewers when she and her mother had first come in to ask for clothes.

I recognized it because I had been regularly purchasing stickers for the interviewers to give to children who came with their parents for food or clothing. Sometimes getting food or clothing at PACS could take a long time, so this was a small distraction for youngsters. It was also a gentle way of introducing children to Christian spiritual concepts, which we hoped might be a comfort to them at some point in their lives.

"What is that?" I asked, pointing to the sticker on the back of her tiny hand.

She sat up straight and lifted her hand toward me so I could see her hand. "That's my sticker," she proudly proclaimed.

While touching it gently, I asked, "Do you know Who that is?"

A huge smile suddenly bathed her lips and hollow eyes. Her bruised face lit up, and her countenance softened. After straightening up even taller and then clutching her stickered hand to her bosom as if He were with her in person, she looked into my eyes and said warmly, "That's Jesus!" Then she quickly stood up and scampered back down the stairs to her mother, thus ending our short conversation.

She was just a tiny child already wise beyond her years, but somewhere she had learned to have fuzzy feelings about Jesus. Talking about Jesus, even as a four-year-old, brought her joy and peace. I pray that her experience at PACS has continued to light up her life and help her find safety in her Jesus.

5

CHAPTER

Faith Means It's Already Accomplished

"Oh, Lord," Linda began her prayer at worship that morning, "You know that many people are hungry. You know that many families will be coming today that need food. And You know we're s'posed to give out oatmeal. Lord, these people need something nutritious for their breakfast. Oatmeal is nutritious, and we don't have any. Please send us oatmeal today. We don't need anything else, just oatmeal. Thank you for doing this. Amen."

My heart dropped. This woman exhibited such childlike faith. *God doesn't answer every little prayer, especially for such a simple request,* I thought. In my mind, God welcomed the big problems. He wasn't particularly concerned with whether PACS had oatmeal today. I was amazed at Linda's lack of sophistication and presumption. Then I felt sorry for her. How could this clueless, spunky little lady deal with such disappointment? She obviously expected the Lord to give her boxes of oatmeal before we opened the doors in just five minutes. I shrugged my shoulders. I would have to leave that between her and God.

I mulled the conundrum of Linda's conversation with God in my mind. She had been a faithful fixture at PACS long before I got there, volunteering every day for many years. She was a bit of a puzzle to me, the way she talked so simply and plainly to God. I'd never heard anyone pray like her. She lacked any sort of pretense or fancy wording.

Linda's job at PACS was to plan menus for the food boxes and make sure we had the right food available. A former chef, she enjoyed working with food and was knowledgeable about nutrition. She always had two or three choices of vegetables or other items on the menu so people could customize their orders. On top of that, additional foods were added to round out the menus. Now she needed oatmeal, and she was about to be disappointed. I shook my head. How sad.

After worship ended, I made my way back to my office. The day was just beginning, my desk piled high with unfinished projects. Everyone else went quickly to their workstations, including Linda, who was relaxed and smiling. She'd prayed, and all was well. As I settled into my desk chair, I heard, "Come quick. We need help!"

I jumped up and ran downstairs to the parking lot to check out the commotion. There, backed up to the steep ramp leading down into the basement, was a truck ready to unload. And what was in the truck? Yes, you guessed it: oatmeal, and not just a few boxes. The Lord had already provided a pickup truck filled to overflowing and had it sitting outside PACS even while Linda had prayed in worship. We had enough oatmeal for many days, and Linda wasn't the least bit surprised.

Linda didn't surprise easily anymore because she had experienced other times when God had answered her simple, heartfelt prayers. She rarely prayed for her own needs but was quick to pray for the needs of others. She specifically carried a burden in her heart that people would not go hungry. She felt strongly about this and worked tirelessly to help feed people at every opportunity. She was an efficient manager and built a strong food distribution program at PACS. She was very careful about how much money she spent on food through reduced rates at the Oregon Food Bank, and she carefully planned her menus. Linda was a firm believer in eating breakfast, and her menus reflected the importance she placed on having breakfast foods in the food boxes.

Sometimes we struggled to make the money stretch far enough to buy adequate food supplies. Things could get tight, challenging Linda's creativity in planning menus. And sometimes she came up against dead-ends. Such was the case one day as she planned for the day. She'd planned for cereal to be put in the boxes, and yesterday they'd given out the last box we had in our cupboards. She realized the situation was desperate. "Oh, Lord," Linda prayed as she sat in her office early that morning, "we're out of cereal, and there are many families coming to us today. Should I buy some? It is so expensive. Please send us some today, if it is Your will. Amen."

It was before opening time—a busy time for Linda. She went about her duties and then listened to her phone messages. "This is Trader Joe's" a voice said. "I know this is not the day we usually give you food, but we have too much cereal. Can you send someone to get it right away? Send a truck or something because we have 240 boxes."

What did Linda say? "Hallelujah, praise the Lord!" Then she quickly dispatched a puzzled truck driver, who was surprised to go to Trader Joe's on an unscheduled day.

Linda's faith was confirmed once again, and my faith grew exponentially as I watched her confidently walk with her Jesus.

6

CHAPTER ═══════════════════════════

Difficult, Heart-Warming Work

Volunteering at PACS can be a traumatic yet heart-altering experience. New volunteers are invariably excited about their work. Every day is a new, exhilarating experience. It is heartwarming and satisfying to be able to help people in need. Sometimes people need clothes, sometimes they need food, sometimes they need health care, and often they need everything. They always appreciate a warm smile and a listening ear.

But after a while, in most of the volunteer's experience at PACS, the golden hue of helping people begins to tarnish. First, helping people is emotionally taxing and physically tiring. Second, helping people is hard, especially if they come with a sense of entitlement and thanklessness. Third, some people are downright dishonest, attempting to deceive the volunteers into helping them when they don't need it. No one likes to be duped.

At times like this, new volunteers sometimes become disillusioned about helping people. The ethical dilemma of continuing to help when it isn't appreciated, or willingly putting oneself in a position to be possibly duped, begins to wear on the mind of the volunteer. We watched closely for these times in a volunteer's experience.

The clues usually came in the form of head-scratching thoughts. "Is there anyone who really needs help out there, or is everybody scamming the system?" "Why don't people get jobs?" "Some of these people wouldn't need help if they cleaned up their lifestyles." "The cars they drive are better than mine." "All these people are on welfare, just leeching the system."

When we heard these questions or observations, we knew this was a time of transition. The volunteers were now grappling with the spirituality of responding to Jesus's call to love their neighbor. We think loving our neighbors will be easy and fun, always rewarding, always satisfying, and always appreciated. And sometimes that's exactly the way it happens. But the reality is much of the time, loving our neighbors is hard, unappreciated, and frustrating.

This is a huge hurdle for many volunteers. I believe it is one of the reasons God calls us to enter this world of chaotic unpredictability. It's hard to find ourselves in the world of hard-living people, especially if that has not been our experience. It's hard to stay there, hard to understand things that don't make sense, and hard to love the unlovable.

When a volunteer's experience became a time of struggle and deep soul searching, this opened opportunities for sincere and serious discussions. Sometimes volunteers could not make the transition, but fortunately most of them did. In a successful transformation, the volunteers would slowly gain a new frame of mind and a maturing of their spirituality, leaving the unanswerable questions with God, trusting Him, and learning to accompany His children in whatever way they were allowed.

Then we knew the volunteers would stay because their loyalty had switched from helping the agency to serving God in whatever way He called. Then it would not matter whether their friends quit volunteering or their supervisor changed. They were taking the first steps toward learning to truly love, feeling God's compassion move their hearts in unforgettable ways. Then they were at PACS for the long haul because their hearts were intertwined with the call of God for His people.

One of the times when volunteers' hearts would be particularly touched was when they encountered children in need. Though many stories were recounted through the years, one volunteer told how helping a child impacted his heart.

This volunteer was a truck driver who worked day and night, even on the weekend. He and another volunteer usually worked together, and this weekend was no exception. They made their usual rounds to pick up bread from grocery stores, unloaded the bread back at PACS, then packed the truck with furniture from PACS to deliver to a family in need.

I've kept the truck driver's story intact, using words he approved when he proofread it for an article published several years after this happened.

"One Sunday, we went down to a two-bedroom house, and we went in. They had a wooden spool for a kitchen table, a few dishes in some apple boxes for a cupboard, a pile of clothes, and no beds. We took them a nice breakfast set, davenport, recliner chair, end tables, and a full-sized bed, which we set up.

"There were three kids, a boy of about seven and two girls of about four and eleven. I said, 'Where do you want the bed?'

"The mother said, 'Put it in this bedroom, here.'

"The oldest girl said, 'Mister, is that really going to be my bed? I never, ever, had a bed.'

"Can you figure that? Ten or eleven years old, and never had a bed?"

He clasped his chest, swallowed hard, and quickly blinked his eyes. "Can you imagine what that does to your heart?"

He had been delivering furniture for decades, but this experience stayed with him.

Helping people is hard work, but just when we need it, the Lord opens our eyes to the real poverty around us. This is His reward. Nothing feels better than the satisfaction of being used by Him to make a difference for someone else, especially a child.

7

CHAPTER

Perpetual Pharmacy

D octors become very frustrated when they prescribe medication
but patients can't afford to get it. This is often a major problem
in free health clinics. It is discouraging for medical personnel and
patients alike. Some doctors avoid volunteering their time in free
health clinics because when a diagnosis needs follow-up, whether
medications, referral to a specialist, or a surgical procedure, the
patients can't afford to get the treatment. Practicing this kind of
medicine seems pointless and unfulfilling.

Fortunately, Portland Adventist Medical Center, a three-
hundred-bed hospital nearby, provided follow-up care to our
patients at no charge. PACS also had agreements with other
healthcare entities for conditions not covered at the Adventist
Medical Center. In addition, the PACS Family Health Clinic had a
room designated as a "pharmacy" for free samples we received from
many generous doctor's offices or pharmaceutical representatives.
This made the PACS Family Health Clinic a satisfying place for
doctors to volunteer, and it helped provide well-rounded care for
our patients.

Having a "pharmacy" necessitated specific expertise in handling medications. It had to be organized appropriately, and medicines had to be rotated regularly with great attention to expiration dates. When I first came to PACS, Dr. Hoffman, a retired missionary and anesthesiologist, volunteered to keep the pharmacy organized. He spent countless hours arranging the medicines, shelving the good and discarding the outdated. He was acutely aware of times when we ran out of different types of medicine, especially antibiotics. One day he told me, "I sometimes worry when certain medications run low, but every time that happens, God impresses someone to donate just what we need." This was a truism that played itself out over and over.

Early one morning, I went through the mezzanine outside my second-story office, crossed the hall that served as the clinic waiting room, and entered the clinic. To my left was a small receptionist desk located just under a sliding window. To the right was the nurse's desk. The clinic had three exam rooms with the doctor's desk set on the wall between the second and third exam rooms. At the very end in a small closet was the pharmacy. All of this was in the north end of a very large gathering room. The space was bright and open.

As I entered the clinic, I found the nurse at her desk taking things out of a small paper bag. "What is that?" I asked quizzically.

"I'm not sure," she replied. "I think someone left it here after closing time last night. It looks like pills and medications. It's probably some antibiotics or something donated from one of the doctor's offices." I watched as she pulled out several bottles of medicines, curious to know what was there. She set them out on the desk in front of her.

"These are really unusual medications. They are very expensive, and here are the supplies that go with them. These would only be used by someone who has a specific disease," she stated. "I'm not sure when we would ever use these, but I'll put them in the pharmacy so Dr. Hoffman can log them." With that, she stuffed them back into the paper bag and placed it in the pharmacy.

Later that day, someone without an appointment came to see the doctor. There seemed to be an urgency about this case, so the nurse scrambled to squeeze him into the schedule. After seeing the patient, the doctor came out of the examining room solemnly scratching his head. "This patient is very ill and has no money for prescriptions," he said gravely. "The medicine he needs is very expensive. Nurse, would you please try to find a place that will donate these medicines?"

As the doctor outlined what he wanted, the nurse suddenly remembered. *The paper bag!* she thought. *Everything the doctor wants is in the paper bag that was left on my desk last night!*

"I can get you those things," she told the doctor. "I'll have them ready in just a minute." She opened the bag, double-checked everything, and then handed it to the doctor. She felt a huge sense of awe as she realized the import of that moment.

Where did those medicines come from? We'll never know, but the Lord certainly showed us how to use them.

8

CHAPTER ═══════════════════════════════

Slow to Learn

" **H**ello, this is the Oregon Food Bank. We wanted to let you know that PACS and another agency are assigned to collect food in a local grocery store." They went on to explain this was a new agreement the food bank had with all the grocery stores in Portland. The arrangement was that once a year, starting this year, the food bank would arrange for every food pantry to spend from 8:00 a.m. to 5:00 p.m. in a local grocery store collecting food.

People would buy groceries and then donate some of those groceries to whatever agency was collecting them on their way out of the store. It was scheduled to happen in two weeks on Saturday. We had been assigned to split the donations with the other agency if we would help collect the food during the day.

This was great news because we always needed food, so I accepted the assignment. Normally, on Saturdays our agency is closed, and volunteers who are Seventh-day Adventists observe the day as holy, which may include going to church in honor of the fourth commandment, "Remember the Sabbath day, to keep it holy" (Exodus 20:8 KJV).

I wondered about participating on Saturday, but I knew Jesus did good things on the Sabbath, and I felt this was serving like Him. Others agreed, and before long I had volunteers for the entire day. There were so many people who wanted to help that I did not schedule myself for a time at the store.

The day came. I went to church, knowing everything was well planned and would go smoothly. I looked forward to Monday, when I would find all the food piled upstairs in the meeting room at PACS. Everyone would be thrilled with having additional food to give out.

On Monday, I eagerly ran to the meeting room to rejoice with the volunteers over the food. I looked around, bewildered. Where was it? *Oh, well,* I thought. *Someone probably decided to wait and bring it in after we open. Maybe later in the day, or the next.*

Monday went by, and no food appeared. On Tuesday afternoon, the food bank called me. "We are so sorry you haven't received any food from last Saturday's food drive," they said. "Things just didn't turn out the way we expected, but maybe next year will be better. Anyway, thank you so much for sending people to help."

Puzzled, I called the last person on my schedule for the Saturday food drive. I asked about the food. Evidently, he had not understood the arrangements because he explained, "Your truck from PACS came at 5:00 p.m., and we loaded all the food. No one was there to pick up the food that should have gone to the other agency, so I assumed we were supposed to deliver it all to them." It was a complete mix-up. All the food was given to the other agency. We got nothing.

The next day when I got to work, I saw a bunch of food piled in the meeting room. "What is this?" I asked. "Where did it come from?"

"Oh, a local elementary school decided to do a food drive on Sunday and Monday and donated it all to PACS." The students had collected as much food as we had given away after spending all day Saturday in the grocery store. I realized God did not need my help to accomplish His work. He expected me to keep His day holy, and He would take care of providing food for the hungry. We were glad to be of help to the other agency.

The story could have ended here, but it didn't. The next year, the food bank called again. They felt so bad about us not getting anything the year before that they assigned PACS to a store all by itself. This time, we would not share the proceeds. Thinking this must be providential, I again decided the Lord would want us to do this good thing, even though it would be on Saturday. Again, people who did not get to volunteer for PACS during the week but loved the cause offered to help. They were excited. By the time Friday evening came, everything was organized and ready.

At 10:30 p.m. Friday night, my phone rang. It was the food bank. They called to regretfully inform me that for some reason, the store had just called to cancel the event. The food bank apologized. All the other agencies would be collecting in area stores, but they could not find a store at this late hour for PACS.

Amazed, I put down the phone. I remembered the year before when we had given all the food to another agency. I also remembered another Saturday afternoon when several hundred youth engaged in a food drive for PACS. It was a dismal failure.

Finally, I got it. It took me over two years to learn that collecting food on Saturday was not God's plan for PACS. God could take care of us; He did not need my help. I must trust in Him. I determined PACS would never have another food drive on Saturday while I was executive director, and God always gave us enough.

Admittedly, this story raises some difficult issues. Isn't it good to help people on God's holy day? Even the Bible talks about getting the ox out of the ditch on the Lord's day (Luke 14:15). What about during times of disaster, is it better to sit in church than to help one's neighbor? Why did PACS's plan get foiled twice in a row?

I believe we should help people on the Lord's Sabbath day, especially if there is an immediate emergency. Could it be that routinely laying up provisions on the Lord's Day is different from helping people out of immediate difficult circumstances or relieving pain? I've included this experience to stimulate your thoughts on this subject because I believe it must be between each person and the Lord. Only He can direct us in every circumstance.

9

CHAPTER

Warm with No Coat

I t was early December, rain was the norm, and temperatures were cold. The constant dampness in Portland can chill you to the bone, making a warm fire, a good book, and a steaming mug of hot cocoa the perfect way to spend the seemingly endless, overcast days when darkness comes early. This was one of those days. A blustery winter storm rode a cold jet stream down from Alaska, colliding with tropical moisture from the Pacific Ocean. Today, it was raining hard with an occasional snowflake scattered in. Last night, the storm was heralded by terrific blasts of wind, uprooting trees, cutting off electricity, blowing away shingles, and breaking off huge limbs. Portland and the hills around it are laden with large evergreens that bend and sway under the burden of winds anywhere from forty to ninety miles per hour. These storms are extremely dangerous, causing treetops to snap off, limbs to break, or whole trees to blow over.

The storm raged through the night and then calmed somewhat the next morning as people lined up, waiting for PACS to open at 9:00 a.m. On rainy days like this, water would puddle on our flat roof and leak into the building. The water dripped through the hanging asbestos-tile ceiling and filled up the fluorescent light fixtures. A few well-placed garbage cans caught the water from the ceiling tiles, and a larger garbage can was used to catch the water from the light fixtures. After the fixtures and the garbage cans were emptied, we could let the long line of people come in out of the cold.

The people came in gratefully, shaking off wet umbrellas and blowing their warm breath onto their hands. After they got what they needed, they would sprint for their cars or the bus stop.

John arrived that morning, cold, with no umbrella. He was visibly shaken by the events of the frightening windstorm the night before. "A huge tree fell right on top of our mobile home," he reported. "It barely missed my wife, who was in bed with pneumonia. She managed to escape, but the house is totally ruined. It is smashed. We have no electricity, no heat and no food." He added dryly, "Not that we could cook it if we had any."

"What did you do?" questioned Shirley, the volunteer who was helping him.

"There wasn't much I could do," John replied. "It was raining so hard that the first thing I had to do was find another place where we could stay. Fortunately, we found some temporary housing. We don't have any tarps or any way to keep the rain out of our mobile home, especially with a tree lying in the middle of it. Our clothes, our linens, the furniture—all of it is soaked and ruined. Nothing is left.

"I'm worried about my wife," John continued as he wrung his hands. "We need only a few things for our temporary housing, but she is sick, and we left so suddenly that her coat is still under the tree in the mobile home."

The staff at PACS went into instant action to gather food and help him choose clothing to replenish what had been lost. Finally, the only article he still needed was a coat for his wife. Alas, there was no coat to be found. John was devastated, as were the volunteers, especially Shirley. They were extremely concerned about his wife because she was already ill. John went on his way, and soon it was noon. The doors were closed for business.

After everything was put away and readied for the next day, Shirley prepared to leave. I visited with her a few minutes and told her goodbye. Just then, I noticed she wasn't wearing her coat. I remembered she had been all bundled in a soft, fuzzy coat when she'd come that morning.

"Wait a minute, Shirley," I said. "Let me get your coat for you."

"No, no, it's okay." She held her hand up to stop me. Then she told me softly that when we couldn't find a coat for the wife of the man with the ruined mobile home, she'd given him hers. She gave away her thick, gorgeous warm coat to him, saying, "Here, take this to your wife. May it keep her warm and safe in the love of Jesus." He'd left that day with tears of gratitude, realizing that in a world turned upside down, there still existed love and compassion beyond measure.

"I'll be all right," she said as she waved off my concern and dashed to her car. It had been a good day for Shirley, and she felt warm all over.

10

CHAPTER

The Gift of Understanding

E ach year across the nation, certain cities are designated by the
federal government as port cities to receive a specific number of
immigrants or refugees from explicitly appointed countries. Every
year, those designation allocations are reassessed. The cities may
stay the same or may change, and the countries represented by
the immigrants or refugees may change. The appointed cities are
expected to meet the needs of those coming into the country for
the first time, helping them to integrate and become self-sufficient.
Some agencies are given funds to help cover the costs of integrating
these new people into their communities, but other agencies, like
PACS, respond to the needs because it is the caring thing to do. This
is a massive undertaking as thousands of refugees are assigned to
each city. Depending on the size of the city, thousands of people
are dumped in a place where they don't speak the language or
understand the culture.

For many years, Portland was designated as one of two cities on
the West Coast where many Eastern Europeans and some Asians

were sent upon entering the United States. As can be expected, the sheer numbers of people coming into these port cities created a burden upon all the agencies, regardless of whether the agencies got money from the government.

Most people coming to Portland came with almost no clothes, no food, no furniture, no place to live, no money, no jobs—nothing. They were truly destitute, finding themselves in a large city and often in deplorable living conditions. The Immigrant and Refugee Community Organization, (IRCO) was the lead agency in finding decent housing and furniture. They worked hard and effectively to meet the challenges, and PACS supported IRCO in these efforts.

One of the biggest daily challenges at PACS when serving the immigrants was communicating to Russians who spoke no English. The days were long and hard because the immigrants tried to make their requests known while our PACS volunteers struggled to understand what they needed. We had no translators, so we relied on gestures, facial expressions, and body language. The volunteers felt the strain and prayed together in worship every morning for understanding.

Many times while trying to help someone, a volunteer would send a quick silent prayer heavenward, begging the Lord to help provide wisdom to know what was needed. The assistant director of PACS began to take the lead in serving the immigrants lining up for help. Things seemed to go more smoothly when she helped. Everyone began to smile more as they interacted. To the observer, it looked like they must be understanding each other, but when asked about it, my assistant director told of her personal experience.

"No, I don't know their language. I simply listen carefully and ask the Lord to tell me what they need. The Lord impresses me, and I serve them. Then I pray with them, even though they don't understand English. Many times, it seems like they understand my prayers. They are so appreciative. They are learning how to say, 'God bless you.' I don't know any Russian at all. I never have, and I probably never will. When we are done with prayer, they hug me and leave with all their needs satisfied."

She experienced this gift of understanding many times and became a key person in the city as she supported the immigrants. She went to their homes, learned about their backgrounds, and worked tirelessly to help them settle in their new lives. They learned to trust and rely on her. As they became more proficient in English, many came to PACS just to talk with her. She was able to help them navigate through very difficult times in their lives, and they still love her deeply for the interest she took in them and their families.

She always understated her role, saying she was honored to rely upon the Lord to alleviate the burden of relocating in a foreign country.

11

Left for Dead

The PACS Family Health Clinic started from a dream of several people who longed to provide relief at a deeper level than just food and clothing. This was before the days of national health care availability. It seemed that health issues often precipitated a downward spiral. A person would suffer an injury or develop a lingering illness or a chronic disease, and then the difficulties would mount. Often people with health issues were not able to work, sometimes for extended periods of time. These work absences created difficulties for employers, and sooner or later, a person would be too sick to keep a job, or someone would be found to replace the worker.

At the point they could no longer work, they would be forced to accept disability or some other form of government subsidy, which was never enough to adequately cover the bills or provide food and afford medical care. The first thing people quit buying was usually clothes, because clothing could be worn longer and didn't become a necessity as quickly as having enough food. Many times, people struggled between buying food and medicine. Usually medicine won over food, or people moved to eating cheaper but less nutritious food. Cheaper foods were usually more calorie dense, using fats, sugars, and salts to make the food taste better. This created addictions and obesity, multiplying the health issues faced by people with low incomes. It was a vicious cycle: as people ate less healthfully, they became sicker, and as they became sicker, they ate more poorly.

As part of health outreach to the community, the Walla Walla University School of Nursing began to have their student nurses come to PACS and do health assessments for people waiting to receive food. The student nurses would invariably find people with high blood pressure or some other risk factor, but they couldn't do anything to help the people other than recommend they go see a doctor. Most of the people had no money for a doctor, and there was no state or federal health care available. Soon it became clear a higher level of care was needed. Through a long process, volunteer doctors and nurses began to schedule hours there, equipment was procured, and the dream of a functioning clinic began to become reality.

The clinic was designed to provide primary care, meaning doctors treated all complaints or referred to a network of specialists and other medical institutions that could take over the care of patients who needed higher levels of intervention. One of those institutions was Adventist Medical Center, a local hospital that was a major supporter of PACS. The center did not support with money, but they encouraged their medical staff to volunteer at PACS or accept patients from the clinic at no charge. They also provided labs, radiology, and X-rays at no charge, along with more complex treatments. It was a partnership that was the envy of other free health clinics in town.

The clinic grew quickly and soon was open Monday through Thursday, usually in the mornings staffed by nurses and physicians, and in the afternoons staffed by nurses and a pediatric nurse practitioner. The cases were becoming more complex, the pharmacy was quite well supplied, and systems and referral streams were becoming efficient.

Many cases were lamentable, but one was gut-wrenching.

On this morning, the nurses and physician were seeing the usual entourage of patients. A patient without an appointment walked up to the window. The receptionist, a woman with limited eyesight who never went anywhere without her seeing eye dog, glanced up to see how she could help. She gasped in horror. Later she told me, "Even with my poor vision, I could see a lady who had been totally beat up. I rushed to let her in."

Melody staggered in, supported by a friend. She was immediately ushered into an exam room, and the story unfolded. Three days earlier, her husband had beaten her unconscious, leaving her for dead. Her eyes were swollen, her nose was pushed in and sideways, several teeth were missing, she thought her shoulder was broken, and she was black and blue from head to toe. She had no doctor, no insurance, no money, and nowhere to turn. One look, and the volunteer physician and nurses rallied to get her relief. Melody got instant care and immediate prayer.

The doctor called referral specialists and sent her to Adventist Medical Center for X-rays. Over a period of several months, the specialists at the hospital donated their services to reconstruct her face, fix her teeth, and take care of her other injuries—all at no charge to her. Other volunteers in the Health Clinic set her up with counseling, legal representation, and helped her find shelter and safety from her abusive husband. Together, over the next year, the health clinic staff and the specialists teamed together to help her pick up the pieces of her life without her husband, who was now in jail.

Melody contacted us nearly two years after she was resettled. She was a changed woman. She beamed as she told us how she had accepted Jesus Christ as her Savior and found a new life, new health, and a new purpose. God had provided.

12

CHAPTER ————————————

Seventy-Year-Old Volunteer Graduates

One day I asked my assistant director, "What does it mean to serve the Lord with all your heart, all your soul, and all your strength, like it says in the Bible in Deuteronomy 6:5? What does that look like?"

"That's easy," she replied. "Just watch Sophia. She loves the Lord and serves Him with a single-minded focus that never quits. She fearlessly gets on the bus before 6:00 a.m. every day, well before the sun comes up, and travels to PACS. She goes back to her government-subsidized housing in the late afternoon, briskly passing through rough neighborhoods. She's been mugged twice, once getting only bruises and the other time suffering a broken arm in the scuffle. For years, I picked her up every day. When our schedules changed, she started to ride the bus. She's tiny and vulnerable, but nothing stops her from serving her Jesus."

It was true. Sophia worked nonstop, and she expected everyone else to do the same. We called Sophia our Energizer Bunny because she was so spunky and energetic. She was a petite lady with short, straight, light brown hair shaped in a pixie cut. Her eyes sparkled impishly, and she loved a good joke. On the other hand, whenever something would happen that she didn't like, she was a formidable force. The impishness left, and her eyes shot daggers. Though she never swore, her mouth was quick to let people know when they'd messed up. No one wanted to cross Sophia, yet Sophia had a most endearing charm about her and a special affinity for young people.

Sophia managed a program for PACS related to the court system for offenders who were assigned community service as part of their sentences. Sophia not only managed the program but also supervised the offenders who were assigned to our agency. They were in their late teens to early twenties, young, strong, mouthy, and belligerent. Sophia loved them unreservedly, and they knew it. By the time they finished their court-appointed time, they were without fail respectful and happily obedient. She gave them responsibility, didn't take any nonsense from them, and made them feel important. They would often continue working even after their time was done because they loved Sophia.

Through the years, Sophia's life unfolded in ways she did not expect. One of her disappointments was that she couldn't finish high school. Her lifelong dream was to get her high school degree. By the time I came to PACS, Sophia's dream had faded because by then she was seventy-one years old. She constantly felt inferior to people who had more education.

The fact that Sophia's dream had faded did not lessen the importance of helping her find her dream again. She was plenty smart, and I was convinced there was no reason why she couldn't pass her General Education Development (GED) test and earn her high school diploma equivalency. We talked about it many times, and Sophia began to dream again.

The day came when she went, all by herself, to sign up for GED preparation classes. She enrolled and was given a schedule. It meant that after working at PACS, Sophia rode the bus downtown to school three days a week for several months while she worked on her GED, which covered five subject areas. During that time, she was hospitalized with severe heart trouble, had two cataract surgeries, and volunteered more than 2,500 hours.

The math test frightened Sophia. She didn't feel at all confident with numbers. A local math teacher agreed to tutor her at no charge, giving countless hours of his time to help her become less afraid.

Finally, Sophia felt ready to take the tests. She surprised even herself by passing all five tests with outstanding scores. Sophia's instructor told her she had never had anyone pass every test without retaking at least the math section. Sophia was quick to give God the glory for her success.

Then it was time to plan a graduation ceremony. Sophia's church family wanted to celebrate too, and offered their sanctuary for her graduation service. Her math tutor agreed to give the graduation address, music was planned, and everything would be decorated with flowers and streamers. But we needed a graduation gown. She was graduating in the winter, not when schools were getting gowns. I began privately praying. I didn't tell anyone about my prayer, and no one expected that she would use a graduation gown. But how can you have a real graduation without a gown?

I continued praying. In the meantime, things went on as normal at PACS. We made our graduation plans, and the days passed as usual. Just a week before the big graduation day, I was downstairs sorting donations. While pulling things out of a black plastic garbage bag, I discovered a bright royal blue, never-been-opened package wrapped in see-through plastic. Excitedly, I grabbed it and tore it open. Yes, it was a graduation cap and gown! I ran to show it to Sophia, and miracle of miracles, it fit her tiny frame. It was exactly the right length, the cap fit perfectly, and the blue made her eyes sparkle.

She looked radiant in her royal blue gown as she marched proudly down the long, long aisle of her home church, the only graduate of her class. After the ceremony, everyone gathered downstairs in the church fellowship hall for refreshments and celebration. Sophia's lifelong dream had been fulfilled beyond her wildest expectations, and she had a gown and diploma to prove it. What an awesome God!

13

CHAPTER

Entertainment Center

Before the days of widespread cell phone use, waiting for the doctor seemed like a waste of time. To help ease the wait, the health clinic had a few donated magazines placed in the waiting room. They were nearly always outdated, and the address label to the original recipient was ripped off or crossed out with black felt pen. No one ever complained about these magazines; it was a way to recycle publications, have some reading material for the patients, and save money.

Like most doctors' offices, the patients had to wait for their appointments; sometimes the wait was short, and at other times it could be longer. Since people sat in the waiting room, it seemed wise to take advantage of this time and turn it into educational moments. Instead of providing only reading materials, I thought it would be nice to play educational videos on lifestyle issues, health, and other topics. After all, some of our patients couldn't read, didn't read well, or didn't read English, so something on TV might be better understood and viewed with more interest than reading a magazine.

The problem was that we had no equipment for this—no TV, no VCR, and no DVD player, which were the common media used at that time. The other issue was that we had no money to buy these electronics or an entertainment center to hold it all.

Oh, well, no problem, I thought. *Maybe someday we can find one.* Whenever the thought came, I would put it off to the back of my mind. However, the idea kept percolating in my brain, coming to the surface again and again. One sunny June day, I got up from the chair in my office and headed over to see the clinic coordinator, Pat.

Pat was an energetic, optimistic, and happy soul who was always ready for a challenge. Her friendly, sanguine personality made her the perfect person to set out on a new project. She had come to the clinic as a favor, just to fill in for a few weeks until we could find a permanent person to fill the vacancy, and she ended up staying for three years. She moved the clinic to a new level of organization and was instrumental in attracting additional volunteer doctors and nurses. Among the many things Pat did well was get donations of things we needed, or at least find things at reduced prices.

"Pat," I said brightly, "what do you think of setting up a TV in the waiting area, so our patients can watch something educational while they wait for their appointments?"

"Oh, that's a great idea." She beamed. "We could set it right here and put the chairs around like this." She moved a couple chairs and indicated how the waiting area could be arranged. "I'll see what I can do." She always had good ideas, and her positive enthusiasm was infectious.

Satisfied that Pat would work on it when she had time, I returned to my office. I couldn't be sure, but I suspected a TV, VCR, or DVD player would appear sometime in the next few months, and by then we would have an entertainment center, or we'd figure out how to put the TV on a table. Either way, by Christmas, maybe an education center would be in the clinic waiting room.

About an hour or so later, a young couple came through the ground floor clinic entrance and up the long flight of stairs to the receptionist window located on the second floor. "Hello," said Pat brightly. "How can I help you?"

"We're not sure if we're in the right place, but we have a donation," they answered. "Can we give it here?"

"I'm sorry, they take donations down in the basement. We don't take them here, but I can show you where to go," said Pat. As a way of making conversation, she added, "What do you have to donate today?"

"Well, we're not sure if you can use it. I know you don't sell anything here, but maybe someone would like it. We have an entertainment center with a TV and a VCR/DVD player. There's even a cabinet that holds it all. We're getting rid of it because we're buying a new one."

Pat gave a little cry of surprise. "Oh, my! Absolutely, yes! Can you bring it up here? We were just talking about how we needed one, and we have a place already picked out where it will be placed." She had them deliver it straight to the waiting room, and then they set it up for her.

Pat then came solemnly into my office. "Can you come over to the clinic for a minute?" she asked gravely, masking her excitement. I suspected they were having some sort of problem, so I put aside my project and followed her back toward the clinic. "There's something you need to see," she added, maintaining her very serious face.

"What?" I exclaimed when I saw the complete educational center all set up. "Where did that come from? How did you do that?" I couldn't believe that within an hour, the very thing I had prayed for was set up and ready to run. We hugged and jumped up and down with joy.

Pat was ecstatic, and so were the nurses, the receptionist, and the doctors. We all agreed: the Lord works in mysterious ways!

14

CHAPTER

Dirty Arms Bring Happy Hugs

Nancy had wanted to volunteer for PACS for a long time. She was not naturally an outgoing person, so it took a lot of courage for her to finally come in and see whether she might be useful to the agency. She was a little tentative when I interviewed her but was willing to do whatever we needed. Her shyness was quite normal for someone's first visit to the agency. Some of the volunteers already knew her and greeted her warmly. Yes, she decided she wanted to join the team, so I sent the proper paperwork home with her to bring back on her first day of work.

Nancy dutifully returned with her paperwork. She was ready to be given a task even though, as on every first day on the job, she was a little nervous.

Her job for the morning was to greet people and hand out clothes. This meant she was on the front lines, meeting a myriad of people from nine o'clock until noon. She wasn't down in the basement sorting donations or working behind the scenes in the kitchen—she was meeting people right after they had been interviewed. Some people were pleasant, others were grumpy, some had hangovers, some were under the effects of illicit drugs, others were single individuals trying to eke out a living, and some were families with children. They all had one thing in common: they needed clothes. They came with a slip of paper in their hands, which told Nancy what they needed. The paper had been filled out when they were interviewed during the intake process. The common practice was to ask people what they needed and then give them items based on their responses. It was customary to provide two of each item for each person in the family—for example, two pairs of pants, two skirts, two shirts, two blouses, two pair of underwear—except for coats, shoes, or linens, which were given as items of one each.

This was all new to Nancy, but she caught on quickly. As the day passed, the supervising volunteer removed her from shadowing other volunteers and let her begin to help people on her own. She discovered she was pretty good at it, and even though the people were sometimes a little scary, she began to enjoy interacting with them. *This is not going to be so hard after all*, she thought.

Things went well for Nancy until a dirty, smelly gentleman by the name of Peter came in. He had been drinking, as a lot of people did who lived around PACS. Grimacing inwardly, she approached him to see how she could help him.

"How can I help you, Peter?" she said brightly, reading his name off the slip of paper he gave her.

"I need some clothes," he slurred. "I need pants and shirts." He didn't tell her he came every month for a couple pairs of clothes. Then he wore them all month until he came for more the next month. He had no washing machine, and any money for the Laundromat was routinely spent in the bar next door to PACS, so after he'd worn the clothes for a month without washing them, he genuinely needed something that was clean.

He also didn't tell her he had no access to bathing facilities, but she could tell that without an explanation. She had never been this close to someone who was obviously drunk, was probably homeless, and reeked of body odor, stale tobacco, and alcohol. After gathering up her courage and pretending her nose was not working, she helped him find some clothes. She put them in a bag and handed them to him. "Thanks for coming in, Peter," she said, "Take care now."

"Oh, thank you, thank you," he said warmly. Then without warning, Peter threw his dirty, grimy arms around her, wrapping her in a huge, happy hug. Nancy nearly fainted.

She thought, *Oh, my goodness, this is terrible*, but she was busy and immediately went back to work. She couldn't even stop long enough to wash her hands. Later, Nancy told me, "I think that was perhaps the first day I realized that even though I wasn't rich, I had a lot more than a lot of other people. I didn't ever realize that people were that needy. I never did."

Nancy volunteered for many years after that memorable first day at PACS. She grew in her understanding of God's leading and in her love for people regardless of how they smelled or how dirty they might be. Nancy's heart blossomed like a flower, reflecting the love of Jesus as she faithfully served in His work.

15

CHAPTER

True Story ... Choose Your Ending

Shoulder-length blonde curls framed her round, chubby face and big blue eyes. She stood, naked but for a diaper, in the doorway of my office. While leaning against the doorjamb in the sultry summer heat, she placed one tiny hand on the door and balanced a bare, sweaty foot on top of the other. Her unblinking gaze penetrated deep within me as only a two-year-old could do. I gazed back, both of us transfixed for a few moments. It was a silent encounter filled with boldness and wonder.

She left silently, as quickly as she had come. The heat weighed down oppressively in my non-air-conditioned office, but I couldn't shake the wonder of the moment. Her baby beauty, innocence, and frank openness contrasted starkly with the bleak future I knew might very possibly be hers.

I wondered about her family. *Where was her mom? Did she have a daddy at home? Was she one of the one-in-four children who went to bed hungry every night in Oregon,* as the statistics stated for that year? *When she got tired in the evening, did she fall asleep in whatever corner she happened to find? Did anyone ever put a blanket over her? How old would she be before she got to sleep in a real bed?*

I thought about her future. *Will she escape a childhood of abuse, or even torture? Has she already seen more of life than I will ever know? Will anyone protect her from her brothers, uncles, neighbors, cousins, and all their "friends"? Will she ever learn about Jesus?*

I longed to grab her and hold her tight. I longed to protect her from what I knew might be her life. But I couldn't. Even ignoring the legal and moral implications of snatching her away, she would have feared me, a stranger, taking her away from everything familiar. She would have resisted my efforts to save her from certain danger. I was powerless to help her.

That encounter was many years ago. Still, I wonder ...

Where is that precious child now? Has she become a statistic—a school dropout, a druggie, a teenage mom? Does she go where poor people go to ask for things because she can't afford to shop in real stores? Is she coming back to social service agencies like the one where I first met her, to feed and clothe her own babies? Has she learned that accepting welfare is preferable to earning a living? Are stealing, lying, and selling her body necessary methods to keep the rent paid, food on the table, and the bail paid for her boyfriend? Do these methods of coping seem so normal that she has no moral aversion to doing whatever it takes, even if chunks of her life are spent in jail? Has she ever met Jesus?

I'm haunted by the memory of that hot summer day when that beautiful child stood in the doorway of my office. What would happen to her and so many other children like her who live in a world of violence, anger, inconsistency and insecurity? What about those children who grow up thinking their chaotic and unpredictable worlds are normal? What about when they become parents, blindly raising their children in the same worlds of violence and cruelty? Will they ever meet Jesus? My arms ache to rescue them, but I cannot.

I once used this story to write a fundraising letter, asking for help to put a happy ending to stories like this. It was one of the most successful letters I ever wrote. It could be a simple story which helped children in distress, but it is more. Somehow there is something about this encounter that strikes a deeper, more personal spot in my heart.

I continue to muse ...

This time, my reverie takes me to a text in the Bible, to words spoken by a deeply distraught parent: "How often I have longed to gather your children together, as a hen gathers her chicks under her wings, but you were not willing" (Matthew 23:37 NIV). Our heavenly Father longs to rescue us, His children, from a world of sin and distress. Just as my arms ached to rescue my visitor that day and all the other children like her, His arms ache to hold you and me tight. Is He more than a stranger to us? Will we push Him away because we don't know Him, or do we trust Him enough to let Him take us away from the worldly things that seem so comfortable? I wonder ... *Have I really, really met Jesus? What will I choose as the end to my own story?*

16

CHAPTER ══════════════════════════════

Dying with Dignity

Tatiana and three other Russian women originally came to Portland on visitor's visas. They never intended to return to their home country because they were looking for a different life. However, a visitor's visa was only good for a few weeks, so people who came on that pretense had to find another way to extend their stay.

Tatiana's three friends soon found Americans to marry, which meant they could legally stay in the country. Tatiana didn't want to marry anyone, but she had no intentions of returning to Russia. When her visa expired, she stayed in Portland, but she could not legally get a job to support herself. She lived alone, finding odd jobs and supplementing her meager existence with food and clothing from PACS. Because of her friendship with Adventists from PACS, she was baptized into a local Seventh-day Adventist church.

Life moved along quite well for Tatiana, marked with ups and downs depending on her ability to find steady work. She remained friends with the other three women who accompanied her to the United States. All four of the women were highly educated professionals in Russia, but they were unable to hold equal positions in the United States without extensive additional education and testing.

One day, Tatiana came to PACS just before closing time. She wanted to see her trusted friend, a staff member of PACS.

"Mary, there's something wrong with me," she confided. "I've been trying to work, but I just don't feel well, and I have so much pain. I can't go to the doctor because I don't have any money."

Mary and Tatiana were good friends and Mary could see that Tatiana did not look well. "Let me help you," Mary replied. "We have a health clinic upstairs, and they will see you, if you're willing. It won't cost you anything, and they have the best doctors and nurses in town."

"Please, anything," Tatiana replied. "I need all the help I can get. I'm so tired, and the pain is sometimes unbearable." Mary immediately took her upstairs to the clinic.

The doctor was finishing with the last patient for the day, and the clinic was preparing to close. When Mary appeared with Tatiana, the nurse was able to quickly put Tatiana in an exam room. During the examination, Tatiana told the doctor a little more about the pain in her side. The physician also noticed Tatiana was obviously very jaundiced. The doctor made a brief assessment and called a specialist to schedule an immediate appointment that afternoon. After filling out the necessary orders, the doctor also sent Tatiana to Portland Adventist Hospital for testing, so the specialist would have test results ready for the appointment. The tests confirmed the Family Health Clinic doctor's suspicion of advanced pancreatic cancer.

A team immediately formed to support Tatiana in her medical care. The health clinic was part of the team, and others involved were the specialist, the hospital, and her church. PACS provided the initial diagnosis, which was followed immediately by extensive surgery for Tatiana. The specialist and the hospital partnered to make this treatment available for her. Tatiana's surgery was followed by more surgeries and nearly seven months in a convalescent hospital. She was so sick that she didn't have the capacity to even worry about how she would pay for this. She barely understood that the hospital provided all this free of charge. This was complete charity care on their part and went much further than our original agreement to provide labs, radiology, and X-rays for PACS' patients. We were touched and gratified by the compassion of the specialist, the hospital, and the caregivers involved in her treatment.

When her church learned of the gravity of her illness, they brainstormed about how they could help and visited her regularly throughout her illness. They sponsored Tatiana's daughter to come from Russia during the months of surgeries, convalescence, and gradual decline. This was a huge comfort to both Tatiana and her daughter, who was able to remain until just a few short weeks before her mother passed away. The church compassionately supported Tatiana as best they could through the most difficult and final days of her life.

It takes a team to provide wraparound compassion in many situations. There is no better way to respond to God's commission to love our neighbors, and there's no better way to create complete unity between God's people than to respond collectively to a person in need.

17

CHAPTER

Disaster Hot Line

We were weary of the rain, which fell day after day. When would it quit? The gloomy January skies seemed to be forever dark, and the weather was cold. The weatherman never seemed to have good news, and today was no exception. Instead of forecasting sunshine as a relief to the rain, he announced that temperatures would drop to single digits, and we could expect snow on top of the already saturated ground. Sure enough, nearly a foot of snow fell overnight. The temperatures remained cold, guaranteeing the white blanket of freezing snow would be with us for weeks.

Northwest Oregon is said to be one of the hardest places in the world to accurately forecast the weather. It is also a place where, if you're a local, you learn to recognize some weather patterns as rather predictable. One of those weather patterns is several days of extreme cold immediately followed by rain. The rain originates high in the clouds where it is warm, but then it falls into a zone of freezing temperatures trapped on the ground, changing from warm rain to freezing rain, and it covers everything with ice. Sometimes the transition from freezing rain back to warm rain happens quickly, and the ice dissolves rapidly. Other times, the ground temperature can remain freezing, and more ice builds up before warm rain breaks through and melts it away. The locals call this phenomenon a silver thaw. These are the days schoolchildren eagerly anticipate because the whole city is immobilized, and everything is closed.

This year was no different. Two inches of ice built up on the snow already covering the saturated ground. One could easily walk on the ice if one could keep from slipping and sliding. Small animals such as mice and rats darted here and there, exposed by this layer of ice instead of being able to scurry through the grass. After the huge buildup of ice, the freezing rain turned to regular rain, and the thaw began in earnest. It rained hard, but there was no place for the rain to go. It flowed off the ice and into the rivers. Small streams began to rise. The rain melted through the ice. The streams became swollen. The rain, ice, and snow all began to melt. The ground underneath was already waterlogged, so the rain could not soak into the ground as it normally would.

The streams began to overrun their banks. They ran into the rivers, and the rivers began to rise. In a short time, local flooding became widespread, including downtown Portland. The bridges that crossed the large Willamette River, which ran through the middle of town, were closed, and a state of emergency was declared.

Everyone wanted to help. Local Christians turned to PACS to organize relief efforts. Churches sent volunteers to help, and PACS increased the normal agency hours from 9:00 a.m. to noon four days a week to an unprecedented twenty-four hours a day for fourteen days straight. We accepted donations of clothes, shovels, cleaning materials, and other flood-related goods. We packed and sorted feverishly before sending them out to a warehouse for distribution. We continued giving out food, clothing, and medical care at the agency. We sent our truck through the floodwaters to deliver food and emergency supplies. We gave tetanus and hepatitis shots, helped fill sandbags, and started a twenty-four-hour disaster hotline. We got enough volunteers to fill telephone operator shifts for twenty-four hours each day, connecting those who wanted to help with those who needed help. Volunteers worked hard to connect loved ones, as well as to connect people with the help they needed.

One day someone called the hotline and reported, "My friend's house has been flooded, and she needs help."

"What is your friend's phone number?" the disaster hotline operator asked. "I'll call and see what she needs."

The phone operator, a volunteer, wasn't sure how someone who had a flooded house would have a phone line that worked, but he had promised to check on her, and that was the only way he knew how to reach her. He rang the number.

"Hello?" said a woman tentatively.

Surprised and relieved to hear someone, the operator identified himself as calling from the PACS disaster hotline. "Someone reported that your house is flooded and asked us to check on you. Are you okay?"

The woman exclaimed, "Is this PACS? I can't believe it! I'm sitting in a boat in my house, and for some reason the phone decided to ring. It hasn't been working—there's too much water in my house. And now when I answer it, it is someone offering to help. I just can't believe it!"

"Well, don't worry. We will find the help you need," the operator assured her. He then took down her requests. He was able to find help for her, and even though it's amazing to picture someone sitting in a boat inside her house, we all thanked God for His obvious miracle in making a waterlogged phone ring.

18

CHAPTER

Carrie

She leaned into the wind, bracing against the cold, driving rain. Her tattered, torn, and dirty coat gave her the barest hint of protection against the brutal winter evening. In one hand, she gripped a large piece of cardboard retrieved earlier that day from a dumpster. The cardboard whipped in the wind, making it hard to handle. The sun had set long ago, providing a welcome cover of darkness as she searched for a spot that would give her the most shelter against the cold and wet. Undefined danger lurked in the shadows, whether from gangs, druggies, winos, prostitutes, or her husband, who always seemed to know how to find her.

While clutching her piece of precious cardboard close, she finally chose a spot she hoped would be safe and dry. Her cough seemed to come more often, and hunger pangs swept over her. Exhausted, she collapsed on her cardboard bed to wait out the dark and stormy hours until morning. Sick, tired, and frightened, she shivered in the dark and reflected on how she had come to be here.

The memories were jumbled, some good and many painful. She thought of her youth, a time of happiness and adventure. She had dreamed of being an author. Even now, her thoughts often strayed to how she might write of her experiences in this bizarre existence. She shivered against a particularly strong gust of wind, remembering the night when her trusting, naïve world exploded.

Soon after their marriage, her husband came home one evening filled with rage. He'd been doing drugs and drinking. She tried to reason with him to find out what was wrong. He became violent, hitting her over and over until she had huge welts and bruises all over her body. Mercifully, he finally passed out, his drunken form crumpled on the living room floor. Crying and bewildered, she nursed her wounds and fell into bed.

Soon it became a regular pattern for her husband: get drugs and alcohol, come home, beat her up, and pass out. She suffered from bruising, progressing to broken bones and finally major internal injuries. Trips to the emergency room were common, always with stories carefully crafted to cover how her injuries were received. She became wary, trying to make sense out of the horrific chaos in which she existed. *Still*, she ruminated, *he is a good man. He's kind, thoughtful, and very compassionate except for those times when he is so drunk and violent. If only I could learn how to be a better wife, then he would treat me better.*

Again, memories of her childhood surfaced. This time, the memories were dark and sinister. She remembered repeated times of physical and sexual abuse, both as a child and an adult. She had learned well the lesson that women were often demeaned, slapped, and exploited, and she prayed daily for the strength to accept her fate as a good woman should. She had learned that a good partner always stuck with and backed her man, no matter the circumstances or how he may treat her.

She felt guilty for running away in the wee hours of the morning while her husband snored in a drunken stupor. She wondered what he would think when he realized she was gone again, and she envisioned him looking for her in her normal hiding places. Maybe she should return, but she still hurt from the last beating, barely able to walk. She remembered the murderous rage in his eyes, and she feared for her life.

While shivering in the darkness and hugging her piece of cardboard, she finally drifted into a cautious sort of sleep, startling like a cat at every noise, in constant vigil even while her exhausted body rested. As the long night gave way to the first faint wisps of light, she made a resolution: she would find help.

And so Carrie made the first of many treks to PACS, where she was warmly greeted, fed, helped to find new housing, and given proper medical care for injuries suffered at the hands of her husband and other men in her life—injuries that would remain lifelong medical concerns. Armed with warm blankets and household articles she was given at PACS, she deftly turned her new, tiny, transitional housing motel room into a cozy home.

As Carrie began to heal, she started coming to PACS every day to find companionship and volunteer in any way she could. She learned quickly, was capable and willing, and soon was managing the fledgling thrift ministry of our agency. As she became more involved and shouldered more responsibility, her eyes lost some of the dazed bewilderment. She startled easily, and her eyes darted here and there, always alert to unknown or unexpected danger. As she became more secure, she relaxed, and after a few months she began to show curiosity about the God of her "angel," as she called her favorite person at PACS. She was a frequent guest in my home and the homes of other volunteers. We took her to the beach and to a women's retreat, and we included her in our very lives. We loved her as best we knew how. She blossomed into a beautiful, charming woman and eventually became baptized, dedicating her life to following her blessed Jesus.

Then one day, everything changed. Carrie did not come to work but left a note saying she was going to move to the East Coast with her husband. He promised to love and cherish her and never beat her again. She was ecstatic with the thought of a new and wonderful life. Knowing the dangers she faced, we were devastated and prayed earnestly for her safety.

I was inexperienced in dealing with cases like Carrie. I didn't know this was a typical pattern for women who experienced control, manipulation, and abuse. I couldn't imagine someone willingly returning to a situation that could be life-threatening, or the bizarre patterns of thinking that abused women embraced. "He said he was sorry—he even cried about it." "He begged me not to leave. He promised that if I would just come back things would be different." "It's not him; it's the sickness … the drugs … the alcohol." "He's a really good man, loving, tender, and kind. He wants our marriage to work." "It's my fault that he gets mad. If I could just somehow be kinder and more caring, he wouldn't do these things."

Some women think in spiritual terms. "When I can learn to be more like Jesus, my husband will change." "If I leave him, my Christian influence will be gone, and he will never be converted." Thus, many women return to abusive situations again and again, even though each time they return, the situation often becomes even more dangerous. Many women have lost their lives believing this faulty thinking.

Two years later, my phone rang. A strange voice identified himself as a pastor of a church on the East Coast and asked if I knew Carrie. "Why, yes!" I responded eagerly. "How is she?" Then the unfortunate story unfolded. Carrie was found on the side of the road by the police, huddled, bloody, severely beaten, and literally freezing to death. Barely coherent, she remembered a birthday party in her honor that had ended in a violent drunken brawl. Once again fleeing for her life, she ran down the highway, waving frantically for help until she collapsed. When the policeman found her, she asked to be taken to a church, told them about PACS, and asked them to call me.

"She wants to come back to you," the pastor said. "Would you be willing to send the money for a bus ticket?" I agreed, and Carrie boarded a Greyhound bus bound for Oregon.

Two weeks later, I picked her up and took her home. Once again, she had that hunted, wary, appearance—a return of her previous symptoms of post-traumatic stress disorder (PTSD). As she showered, bathing in the healing of the warm water, I prepared her a simple, nourishing meal. She was obviously not well, so after she bathed and ate, I took her to the emergency room. While there, the doctor asked her if she ever felt like harming herself. To my surprise, her answer was yes. "In fact," she continued, "I took a shower at my friend's house tonight and looked through her medicine cabinet to find enough pills and medications to kill myself, but she didn't have anything."

When I heard Carrie tell the doctor about her attempt to commit suicide while I was opening my heart and home to her, I was surprised and angry. It was not the first time Carrie had taken advantage of the love we'd extended to her. People had warned me not to send money to bring her back to Oregon. They felt PACS had done enough for Carrie, whose life seemed to be a roller coaster from one episode to another. Most of the time she seemed able to think normally, but other times her thought processes baffled us. We were unwittingly sucked into her drama. We often felt helpless, but we persisted. The only thing we knew was to keep loving her, surrounding her with safety and prayers.

Carrie was admitted to the hospital for further medical care, and when she was discharged, she was set up once more with a room in government housing. Again, PACS furnished her with everything she needed; she gathered a few plants to make it feel like home and managed to find a computer. When her dearest friend from PACS and I visited her a few months later, she proudly showed us her luxurious plants and her tidy, comfortable room. She told us of the friends she had made. She was using her computer to publish her own newsletter, thus fulfilling her childhood dream to be an author. Most important, she was once again sparkling with energy and enthusiasm. She beamed when she talked of how she loved Jesus, and she felt comforted by the knowledge that angels surrounded and protected her.

As I left her and walked out of the government housing building, I prayed for her welfare and for Jesus's blessing on her simple, childlike faith. Upon reaching the curb, I walked around the car and, deep in thought, slowly opened the driver's side door. I gazed up at her third-floor window. *You may never see her again*, I mused. I was wrong.

A year or so later, Carrie stood in my office door. She was battered and upset. After greeting and hugging her, she stated the reason for her visit. She didn't need anything; she simply wanted to visit her dear friend who worked at PACS and who had been her role model. On the way, Carrie had been mugged. Sadly, the friend she had come to see no longer worked at PACS. Once again, we helped her as best we could, prayed with her, and bade her goodbye. My heart yearned after her, but my mind said, *This is truly the last time you will ever see her.*

And I was right.

How hopeless some cases seem, and how helpless we often felt in trying to support Carrie. This is a common feeling, and often it's used as an excuse for not getting involved with people who confuse or frighten us. We didn't understand the connections Carrie had already developed with other government agencies, who supported her by providing housing, medical care, and other needs. This was a huge help that we could not have provided. In retrospect, if I were to do this over, I would have reached out to her case workers to try to provide a more seamless, wraparound approach for Carrie's life. On the other hand, perhaps all God wanted us to do was to love her without judgment or expectations. One thing I do know: through this experience, the Lord opened my heart and gave me immeasurable blessings of learning to love unconditionally, even when rebuffed or mistreated. We did what we could and left the rest with God.

The end of the story. Sometime later I happened to find one of Carrie's newsletter articles online. In it, she carefully described her experience. I recognized her story, having known and experienced many of the details with her. She glowingly described how her "angels" had helped her and literally saved her life. I was gratified that she appreciated the sacrifice and love she had received, though it puzzled and disappointed me that she never mentioned PACS by name. Only at the end did she give credit to her "angels," which she declared were located at Salvation Army. It hurt. *Why should they get the credit?* The Lord taught me many things through helping Carrie, and He had one more lesson. Through a surprising and somewhat comical twist in Carrie's thinking, He protected me from the arrogance of thinking we had made a difference for Carrie. We were simply His avenues of love for her. I suspect she will someday bask in the eternal warmth of His gaze and the safety of heaven, and I'm anxious to meet her there.

PART TWO

PACS Moves

Rules Changed to Provide Dignity and Allow Freedom of Choice

19

CHAPTER

Décor Matters to God

Everyone was excited because moving day had arrived. The entire agency closed for two weeks to move into a newly remodeled building all on one floor with lots of parking. PACS had outgrown the old building long ago, but we'd limped along. The old building was three stories, with a daylight basement, a ground level floor, and a second story. The roof leaked, one of our clients had run a car through the basement windows, and the parking lot had space for only five automobiles. We'd sold the building without a place to go and had been renting it back for seven months. It irked me to pay rent for a building we used to own.

I constantly searched for another place. Every night until dark, all summer long, I searched. The staff often accompanied me, but nothing seemed right. One day a volunteer suggested we consider looking at a building for rent near her house. We didn't want to rent, but we checked it out. It was once a grocery store and most recently was a fitness gym with a daycare facility. It would need some remodeling, but it had the basics we needed. It was in a part of town that had the highest number of free school lunches being served, and it was right by a bus stop.

The owner said he'd consider selling it and gave us permission to have a combined staff and board meeting in the empty building one afternoon. We stood in the building and prayed. We looked it all over and prayed some more. The owner was firm at one million dollars, which was a fortune for an agency that struggled to meet expenses every month. The board and staff agreed to get a loan so the building could be purchased and remodeled. In due time, the loan was approved, and we got ready to move.

Now everything was packed. There really wasn't much. Most of the furniture wasn't worth moving, but it was all we had, so we took it with us. We didn't have money to buy new furniture. We moved some of the clothing racks we'd used in the old building, but they collapsed in the parking lot before they could be carried inside. We were taking the opportunity to change our clothing service into a thrift store format, and we had already found racks and store fixtures for ten dollars each from a J.C. Penney store that had closed.

We were also changing our food distribution program from handing out food boxes to letting people shop grocery-style, without money. We found rusty grocery carts behind a warehouse downtown and bought twenty carts for ten dollars each. A new grocery cart would have been more than a hundred dollars, so we were pleased with our purchase. We cleaned up the carts and painted them silver, and they looked very nice. I learned over the ensuing years that grocery carts are a rotating asset. We started with twenty carts, and a year later we still had about twenty carts, but they were from every store around us. People would come with a cart they'd gotten somewhere else, shop at PACS, and then leave with one of our carts. We never had to buy carts again, even though we routinely returned the carts that had other stores' names on them.

Dan, the moving supervisor, organized the transition. He bustled about and had nearly everything moved and set up before the official moving day. He reluctantly loaded up our beat-up shelves and cupboards. At the last minute, Dan decreed the dilapidated health clinic waiting room furniture had to stay behind. It was simply too rundown, ugly, and rickety. I understood his reasoning, but I knew we didn't have the money to replace it. I'd also learned that when one of my most dedicated and trusted volunteers said no, I'd better listen. The day was so busy that I didn't have time to object, so I left the problem of no clinic waiting room furniture to be solved later.

We moved in. It was a hot, sunny day in Portland, over 105 degrees. We worked hard, and finally it was finished. The building was beautifully remodeled, freshly painted and clean. The teal carpets, slightly mauve walls, and green doors and trim were such a treat after the dark, dingy building we'd left. As the work tapered off, I took the luxury of wandering into each room and savoring the newness.

I entered the shared waiting room of the interviewing area and the health clinic. The new waiting room sat empty. It was gorgeous, newly painted, carpeted where people walked, and tiled decoratively around the edges where we would someday put chairs and end tables. People would have to stand for a while until we could get some furniture. We still had a couple days to settle before our official grand opening.

The next day, a local doctor's office called. "We're remodeling our office," they said. "We'd like to donate our old furniture to you. It's in good shape; we're just changing things out. Our doctor can deliver it this afternoon, if you can use it."

Use it? Absolutely! Even though I hadn't seen it, I knew we would use it no matter what it looked like.

Chairs, tables, and lamps were soon arranged in the waiting room. It was just enough to fill the space, and every piece exactly matched our color scheme. We couldn't have done better if we'd had it special ordered. I was so used to accepting whatever came and using it no matter what it looked like, and I was overwhelmed at the kindness of God. He not only gave us what we needed but went the extra mile to make our new building a respectable place for His work.

We used that furniture for many years, and every time I saw it, I thought of the text in Luke 12:27 (Berean Study Bible): "Consider the lilies, how they grow: they neither toil nor spin, yet I tell you, even Solomon in all his glory was not arrayed like one of these." And we didn't even have to ask.

20

CHAPTER

Food for an Aching Heart

Bob was a retired navy seaman and was proud of it. He liked to act gruff and tough, but his heart was marshmallow soft. Sometimes he reminded me of a big teddy bear even though he had a bark that could be formidable. We didn't always agree on things, but we always managed to work it out. He worked in the food department, stocking shelves, ordering food, helping customers, keeping records, and doing anything and everything that needed to be done.

Bob and I came to PACS at nearly the same time. He came while I was gone on a mission trip. When I returned, Bob introduced himself to me. "Hi, I'm Bob. I work here," he said gruffly.

"Hi, I'm Rhonda," I replied, shaking his hand. "I work here too." And so began many years of service at PACS for Bob and me.

In the next few years, PACS went through a time of transition. We not only moved to a new building but also changed how we gave out food. We studied this change for many months, planning the best way to move from packing food boxes to putting food on shelves in a grocery-style format so people could choose their own. Bob was not so sure he liked the idea of this new format. He voiced his concerns as he became more involved with the food department. He was an important part of our staff, and we appreciated his skills. As we neared the time to move and start the new style of food distribution, he became increasingly troubled.

Other volunteers also struggled with the thought of making this change. Letting people choose their own food removed a certain amount of control, which left the volunteers unnerved. What if the people didn't choose wisely? Even though we developed shopping lists based on a balanced diet, it was difficult to think that people who sometimes made what seemed like unwise choices in other areas of their lives could be trusted to choose what the volunteers felt was nutritious and wholesome.

As his apprehension mounted, one day Bob came to me and declared, "I will help you with the new grocery distribution on the first day. I know you'll need help then, but after that I'm finished. You can find someone else because it's not going to work."

By this time, I knew Bob quite well, and he meant what he said. To have Bob leave at such a critical time would be very detrimental to our program. But I also knew begging him to stay would not be helpful. He had already heard all the reasons for changing, such as preserving the dignity of our clients, not having to clean up unwanted food the clients took out of their boxes and left at the bus stop, and helping people learn how to make small choices and gain back some control over their lives, which were dominated by authoritative systems. He had participated in discussions about how God regarded the option of choice so important that He still allowed Adam and Eve to make the wrong choice at the Tree of the Knowledge of Good and Evil in the Garden of Eden. Yes, Bob knew it all, so I merely thanked him for being willing to see us through the first day of the new program delivery.

The first day came. It was extremely busy, even hectic. We wondered how people would receive this new system. No one had ever seen anything like it, so we had extra volunteers on hand to help as personal shoppers, carefully guiding people through the process until they were comfortable finding food on their own. We were overwhelmed at the positive responses we got from our clients. Most people were flabbergasted that they could pick their own food.

Many people said, "You mean I can pick? I can choose my own food?"

An elderly Eastern European woman stood at the door, her head clad in a scarf pulled tightly above her forehead and fastened behind her neck. She had tears streaming down her face. Concerned, a volunteer asked what was wrong. "Nothing," she sobbed. "I just can't believe there's so much food, and I can choose from all of it." Our hearts were touched by the outpouring of gratefulness for the opportunity to make their own choices.

At the end of the day, Bob came to me and stated, "If you ever go back to the old way of packing food boxes, I will leave PACS. This has been unbelievable." From that day on, he was a staunch supporter of the new food program.

As Bob served in the food pantry, he became good friends with our regular clients. This is a story he recounted to me about one of those clients.

Bob said he recognized Janine right away; she had been to PACS before for food and clothes. This day she stood alone, crying softly to herself. He asked, "Are you okay? You're lookin' kinda sad today."

Janine managed a tentative smile. The words tumbled out. "I think what I really need more than food today is someone to hold me and pray for me. I'm in the middle of a divorce, and my husband refuses to sign the papers. To make matters worse, the other day I went over to my mother's house and found her dead in her bedroom! I've got nobody else!" Bob wrapped her in his big signature bear hug and held her tight until she could regain her composure.

Sometimes the stories seemed unbelievable and overwhelming. The only place Janine had to turn for comfort and love was PACS, a community services agency. Sometimes the food people need is more than food for the stomach. On this day, Janine needed food for her aching heart. Bob thanked God that he was there for her that day.

Thrift Store Nuggets

The thrift ministry was intentionally designed to distribute clothes and household goods to low-income people in a dignified manner. For decades, the volunteers at PACS had proudly proclaimed that everything was free and no one had to pay anything to get the items they needed. This was also important to our donors when they gave items to PACS, knowing that people were compassionately served.

But somehow, the distribution system was flawed. People were grateful to receive things, but it became obvious some things were ending up in yard and garage sales, turning beautiful, handmade quilts and other items into money to purchase drugs or to send to other family members left behind in the homelands of immigrants. Other people were coming regularly to get things after throwing away what they'd gotten the month before. Each person was limited to a certain number of items each month, such as two shirts and two pairs of pants. Often those limitations became points of heated arguments, and some days the volunteers felt more like policemen than humanitarians.

I believe when a service point becomes a clash point, it's often a symptom of a flaw within the method of delivering the service. People are not usually the problem; most often the problem is in the system itself. When things start clashing or have been clashing for a long time, it is time to step back and take an unbiased look at the problem. That is exactly how the staff and volunteers came to the point of calling a meeting of frank discussion and prayer over the future of the clothing program at PACS.

The Lord had been educating us to look at our work through a different lens. The subject of changing the clothing distribution to a thrift shop delivery system was discussed thoroughly with Gail Williams (real name), who had pioneered the idea in the Good Samaritan Center in Ooltewah, Tennessee. Specifically, she taught us people could come in every day or several times a day if they wanted, rather than once a month under the giveaway model. We liked the idea of more opportunity for ministry in that setting. We also had mountains of clothes we couldn't possibly give away quick enough, which we were packing to send to Adventist Development and Relief Agency (ADRA) to be distributed around the world. At about that time, ADRA began running into distribution challenges and no longer needed our clothes. We didn't miss the extra work and expense of boxing and shipping the clothing to ADRA, but clothing had begun to pile up. It was suggested that perhaps we needed to turn the Lord's blessings into the dollars we so desperately needed to keep our agency financially supported.

Many other pros and cons were discussed until the day came for a formal meeting. There was no consensus among the staff over this issue. Some were adamantly opposed, others were favorable, and a few were undecided. The eight staff members and I chose to meet in a nearby church meeting room in order to take ourselves out of our usual setting and free up our minds to think expansively. We sat in a circle, put up a flip chart, and made two lists. One was the pros of changing to the thrift ministry model, and the other was the cons. Discussion was energetic and frank. Sometimes it was heated and sometimes we all laughed together, but it was always respectful and open. We talked until we had nothing more to say; all observations, concerns, and selling points had been discussed to everyone's satisfaction. While sitting in silence, we knew it was time to pray. The nine of us fell on our knees, with each person being given the opportunity to pray as he or she felt impressed. The agreement was that we would pray and then vote by secret ballot. We'd follow the direction of the vote, whichever way it went.

We arose from prayer and distributed the ballots. The voting finished. Each person folded a little piece of paper with either a no or a yes on it and put it in the little wicker basket. With bated breath, we anxiously awaited the outcome. One by one, I pulled the ballots out of the basket. We began the count and ended up with nine yeses. I was stunned with disbelief. The opposition had been strong and vocal, yet all had voted in favor of changing to a thrift ministry. Only the Lord could have intervened to create such unity among these talented and opinionated individuals. They were fully aware that moving into this ministry would meet a wall of opposition among church members and volunteers still proud of not selling things. There would be many planning meetings, strategizing as to how to move forward while answering the concerns of our donors and constituents. They resolutely determined to follow the Lord's leading and, like the pioneers of old, embraced the journey ahead with firm assurance of the Lord's leading.

Even so, selling things was sometimes a difficult concept to embrace. We reminded ourselves of the story in the New Testament (Luke 18:18–23) about the rich young ruler who asked Jesus what he needed to do to be saved. Jesus's answer that he should sell his belongings and give the money to the poor was inspirational to us, and we embraced it as a biblical concept describing the first thrift ministry, even though there are many deeper layers of understanding to the story. We wondered why Jesus told the rich young ruler to sell his stuff rather than give it away; we were sure his stuff was nice and would have been appreciated by the poor. But instead, Jesus told him to sell it and use the money for the poor.

At this time, the whole agency had moved from an old building not capable of handling something like a thrift ministry to a large, revamped grocery story with a complete storefront of floor-to-ceiling display windows. This move gave us the opportunity to plan for the changed delivery system and make it enticing to customers. Salvation Army gave us a portable dressing room, the floor was carpeted to cover the many rough spots, a cash register and welcoming counter were installed near the entrance, and new lighting was installed to make the store bright and inviting. Over a period of several months, the new thrift ministry became a place where people of all ages, ethnic backgrounds, and economic levels shopped together.

In the early days, a Rolls-Royce was a common sight in the parking lot, leftover from the Bhagwan Shree Rajneesh compound that would soon disband in eastern Oregon. We discovered the spectrum of people who came to shop were much wider than those we had served in earlier years because it was open to anyone, not just the poor. Those who had limited income and took pride in supporting their families without accepting charity were thrilled to find low prices and nice merchandise. We realized this was more than a store—it was a ministry. The following nuggets tell this story.

Harold occasionally came to the thrift store. He did not come often enough for everyone to become acquainted with him. One day, he brought a bag of things. "I went through some cupboards last night," he said. "These were my wife's. I would like to give them to you." He went on. "I have kept everything since she died, but now I want you to have them. I've watched what you do here. I know I can trust you to take care of her things, and the money will be used to help others." A tear slid down his wrinkled, leathery cheek.

Sue came in quite often and was full of energy. "Can I have a free Bible?" she asked one day. "The last time I was here, I got a free Bible for my sister, and she likes it so much I want to see what she's reading."

"I love shopping at your store," quipped Marlene over the phone. "You make it so wonderful. I live on a part-time income, and I cannot afford the other thrift shops. I love your store."

Yes, this was a thrift ministry, and we were making friends every day. People signed our prayer request log and returned to tell us how their requests were answered. People were grateful for being able to afford what they needed without asking for charity. God blessed abundantly.

22

Empty Shelves, Full Tummies

It was exhilarating to feel we were in partnership with God to help those around us who were struggling. But times were changing, and things were getting hard for the agency, just like for those we served. Not only was the economy deteriorating, but changes had been made to the federal welfare system. We were warned by our national headquarters, as well as through news channels, of the expected spike in need of the local people as these welfare changes were phased into practice.

These modifications in the welfare system were becoming reality at the local level, and sure enough, more and more people began to ask for help. PACS was staggering under the load of increased need. The projected 400 percent increase of people who would need help turned into a documented increase of over 750 percent in the number of people who came for help as the realities of a depressed economy and welfare changes clashed. Nowhere was this more pronounced than in our food pantry.

Recently, PACS' new, larger location allowed us to change our food distribution model from giving out food boxes to letting individuals choose their own food from shelves set up like a grocery store. This model of food delivery was an instant hit with our clients, who spread the word far and near that people could now "shop" at PACS with a grocery cart, receiving food that would fit the needs of their families based on guidelines that showcased healthy eating.

Unfortunately, the crumbling economy created a desperate cash shortage for PACS. Monetary donations had plummeted, donations of food and clothing were nearing an all-time low, and donations of furniture were nearly nonexistent. When times are hard, people tend to keep their clothes and furniture, putting off the purchase of new items until better times come.

To top it off, we couldn't get our food allotments increased from the Oregon Food Bank for another year. Policy at the food bank was structured so that agencies received their allotments of food based on the numbers of people they'd helped the year before. These allotments were the bulk of what sustained us. But because of the economy, welfare changes, and our change to a grocery-style pantry, more than twice as many people stood in line than we'd served the year before. The food we got from the food bank was inadequate. We needed more than double the amount we were allotted. A couple of times, the food bank gave us special grants of extra food to help ease the desperate situation, for which we were very grateful, but it seemed like our shelves were bare all the time. The local newspaper even came and did a newscast showcasing our bare pantry, highlighting the struggles of those hard hit by the welfare changes and the economy, as well as the agencies trying to help them. Every morning and sometimes during the day, the volunteers prayed earnestly about the situation.

Even though we had very little food to distribute, the food bank required meticulous record keeping, documenting the flow of food into and out of the agency. We had systems developed and people who kept track of these figures daily. For several months, our accountant noticed the month-end figures of food coming and going did not seem to be accurate. He began to worry that somehow the volunteers were not correctly keeping records.

The accountant showed me his numbers, observing, "See here? Our records say we got in this much food from the food bank and from local stores. But look here. See this? It says that we gave out more food than we took in."

Armed with that information, we talked with the food manager and those who kept records. The accountant reminded them it wasn't possible to give out what we didn't get in. The manager was puzzled because he was sure the documentation system was accurate, and he promised to watch closely.

A couple weeks later, this was his report, "I have been watching how the food flows in and out of PACS every day now for ten days. I've been checking to see whether everyone who needs food is getting enough and whether our record keeping is accurately reflecting the activity in our pantry. This is what I've found.

"Every night when we close the doors to the pantry, the shelves are bare. We can't restock them because we don't have anything else to put out. We've given everything away. Each morning before we open, our truck brings in a little food collected from the local grocers. We put it all out on the shelves, but it doesn't begin to fill them adequately.

"As you know, during the day while we are open, we average more than one hundred families, representing roughly four hundred people, who come and shop the nearly empty shelves. But people always got the right amount of food for their families. I saw their shopping carts were full, and sometimes we even had extra food to give away. No one was ever turned away hungry."

His voice broke. "All these months, and I didn't get it. I didn't realize that every day, the Lord has been multiplying the food on our shelves. We have never had to turn away anyone who is hungry. We've been living a modern-day example of the Bible story, of how our God fed five thousand people with five loaves and two fishes." He referred to a story of a miracle of Jesus found in Matthew 14:13–21.

We were struck with awe over this amazing revelation. Finally, after bowing in a prayer of thankfulness to God, one of the volunteers remarked, "And we didn't even have to stock the shelves—the Lord just kept replenishing things on the spot!"

Yes, day after day for nearly a year, this miracle was repeated over and over. When the next year rolled around, our food bank allotment increased to more adequately match our client load, relieving the pain of inadequate food and empty shelves. The accountant happily made his entries knowing they were accurate, documenting the generosity of God during a time of modern-day desperation.

23

CHAPTER

Ripped Off

Transitioning from a free clothing program to a thrift ministry model was an interesting process. We still gave out free clothing to those who needed it by giving people a voucher for a certain dollar amount, which they presented to the checker at the cash register. That way, no one knew who was shopping with money and who was shopping with a voucher until checkout time. It seemed like a good idea, but it sometimes created lengthy lines at the register. It took longer to ring up vouchers than real money. To relieve the congestion, we opened a second register for vouchers only.

One day, I was filling in on the second register for the regular volunteer. I would take the voucher and the clothes chosen by the customer and then ring up the price tag on the clothes until the total reached the allowance on the voucher. If there were more clothes than money, the customer could choose to return some of the clothes or pay the difference in cash. This worked well until an elderly man handed me his voucher and a huge stack of clothes. I knew this man because he came each month for food and clothing. He and his daughter came to PACS in a very late model sports utility vehicle. This was not unusual because often several immigrant families would buy a vehicle and then share it, with each family using it one day a week.

Requesting a large amount of clothes was not unusual either because many grandparents claimed their grandchildren as dependents. In this case, I knew his daughter, who was still shopping, had also claimed the children as dependents, so the children had been claimed in two separate intake interviews. I decided not to ask questions because I did not want to make the two of them go through the intake process again. I also did not want to cause a conflict that could escalate into a heated confrontation. I knew that culturally for him, direct, face-to-face conflict resolution was considered normal.

The man handed me his voucher, and I started ringing up the clothes while putting them in black plastic garbage bags. I rang up seventy items, reaching a total of fifty dollars and twenty-five cents, nearly completely covered by his free voucher worth fifty dollars.

"You did very well," I exclaimed. "You only owe twenty-five cents."

"No, I don't have money," he responded, refusing to pay.

"That's okay," I said cheerfully. "Out of all these clothes, which one would you like to leave here?"

"I must have all," he stated loudly. "I can have them," he declared, even louder. He began to rant and rave.

Because I knew this was part of his cultural routine, I remained calm and continued to talk softly. "You have two choices," I insisted quietly. "You may either pay me twenty-five cents, or you can choose to leave one of these items for next time." I was curious to see how this would resolve, but I stood firm. The impasse progressed while a line began to form behind him, and people grew impatient.

Finally, he reached into his back pocket for his wallet. He opened it up, revealing a thick wad of fifty- and one-hundred-dollar bills. "Here," he said gruffly, pushing a fifty-dollar bill in my hand.

"Thank you," I replied as I fished forty-nine dollars and seventy-five cents in change out of the cash drawer. I sighed. All that hullaballoo over twenty-five cents when he had a wallet full of hundreds of dollars.

Through this and other experiences, I've learned that many cultures allow for variations of standards, especially of honesty, truthfulness, and deceit.

When the doors opened at PACS each day, families brought with them a set of values, which were sometimes in direct contrast to the values espoused by the staff and volunteers. This created a game of matching wits. For example, the volunteer, who believed deceit was evil, encountered worldviews and cultures that did not share such views. Often the volunteers went home exhausted and feeling ripped off. We frequently evaluated our practices and programs to find ways to minimize the seemingly unending battle. Sometimes our solutions worked, and sometimes they didn't.

What was this daily matching of wits, and why didn't it stop? The underlying reason is simple. The cultures and peoples represented, including the volunteers, had varying beliefs and learned attitudes about life that did not always complement each other. At PACS, these influences met, attempted to merge, and separated again until the next visit. In short, the actions of the people who helped and wanted help were based on very different worldviews and cultures that carried different sets of ethics and values.

For instance, honesty, esteemed as an absolute in the Christian worldview, may be considered a dispensable cultural value, even by some people who claim to be Christians. Some may view honesty as having certain degrees or levels that are suitable depending on the situation, and therefore they were not dishonest. I've found most people embrace honesty as an important value for others but not always a necessity for themselves. In other words, most people believe honesty is mandatory for the other person, but not all people think it is important to be honest themselves, especially if they don't get caught.

It is also important to remember the magnitude of relationships on making ethical decisions. When confronted with moral dilemmas, in the absence of allegiance to God, relationships with others or with the self will nearly always rise to the top as the most important consideration.

PACS is an organization adhering to a Christian theistic worldview, with a distinct set of core values and hidden cultural rules and expectations. The people who came to PACS for help often had a different set of values, along with their own unwritten rules and expectations. To help meet these challenges, PACS held focus groups derived from the various groups of people, asking for their help in shaping programs deemed fair and equitable.

We also tried to help volunteers approach these situations from a broader viewpoint, underlining the possibility that perhaps what they interpreted as a moral dilemma was seen in the eyes of the client as simply business as usual. The client usually wasn't "evil" but was simply acting out of her or his own understanding of right and wrong. It might not change our final answer to the client, but it could help take away the frustration in the interaction.

Though these attempts at solutions helped, nothing was as effective as volunteers who consistently lived their own Christian theistic worldview, based on an allegiance to God. They demonstrated unselfish, nonjudgmental love time and time again. This pure outpouring of the grace of Jesus was often acknowledged and returned by quick smiles and a heartfelt "God bless you" from clients. One young man, caught in generational poverty, returned after a long absence from PACS. He came to announce proudly that he had taken the advice of one of the volunteers, gone to school, now had a job, and didn't need anything. These heartfelt gestures of gratefulness were ample reward for the time and effort expended in navigating the sometimes treacherous sea of varying realities and expectations.

PART THREE

God's Leading

Growing in Service
to God and Man

24

CHAPTER

African Virus Strikes in America

The toddler screamed in pain. He was obviously very sick and running a high fever. Puzzled, Dr. Bechtel gently probed the child's distended abdomen. Nothing made sense about this case. The parents spoke no English but were obviously frantic with worry. They had taken their baby to other free clinics in the city, but for one reason or another, no one was able to see them. Someone had finally referred the family to the PACS Family Health Clinic. The referral documents indicated the family had arrived in Portland just a few days ago as immigrants from Africa.

Dr. Bechtel regularly volunteered at the clinic. He was active in his church, was a dedicated Christian, and believed strongly in the healing power of Christ. He had not been to PACS for a few weeks because he had taken time off to participate in a mission trip to Africa. He spent his time in Africa offering health care to the local people, working with a mission team to bring special skills and treatments to areas where these things were not available.

Today was the doctor's first day back to PACS since his trip. He enjoyed the clinic, the clinic staff, and the patients. He was also very appreciative of the professional relationship he enjoyed with the nearby hospital, Portland Adventist Medical Center, as a respected member of their medical staff.

Dr. Bechtel was concerned about the intense pain this child was suffering. The eighteen-month-old baby exhibited extreme symptoms too exaggerated for simple digestive distress. This had to be something different. Suddenly, he remembered he had seen cases like this in Africa. It all became clear. This baby was suffering from what looked like typical digestive distress, but in Africa this type of illness could be caused by a virus. It was extremely serious, and if not treated, it may result in perforated bowel and death. There was no time to lose—the child was in crisis.

Dr. Bechtel called Adventist Medical Center to tell them the child was on his way. In the meantime, the nurse gave directions to the sponsor of the family on how to find the hospital emergency room. Fortunately, it was the closest hospital, just four miles away. It would be quicker to drive than to wait for an ambulance. The family rushed out the door. While the family traveled, Dr. Bechtel briefed the emergency room staff on how to confirm his suspected diagnosis and the treatment that would be required.

The sponsor drove frantically to the emergency center, where staff met the family and rushed them into a room. The medical staff and nurses were ready to take blood and do vitals to quickly confirmed the diagnosis. Dr. Bechtel was right: this baby was suffering from a life-threatening illness that normally would have taken doctors in the States a long time to discover. They had never seen this disease and would likely never see it again unless they traveled abroad, as Dr. Bechtel had.

The surgery suite was immediately cleared for the baby. All hands prepped quietly and intently; the mood was hushed, serious, and quick. No preparation was left undone, but no seconds were wasted because everyone knew time was critical. A baby's life was at stake. Quick prayers ascended to heaven for this precious toddler and his anxious parents. The surgery began.

After what seemed like a long time, the surgeon finished his work, and the operating room staff breathed a collective sigh of relief, offering prayers of joy and thanksgiving. The doctor stepped into the waiting room to meet the sponsor and the parents. With the help of translation through the sponsor, he told them, "Your son survived the operation. His intestines were on the brink of bursting, but through quick intervention and the blessing of God, he is going to live. He is very ill and will need to stay in the hospital for a few days, but he will get well soon."

After a brief stay in the recovery room, the anxious parents were allowed to see their dear son. He was sleeping peacefully—no more pain and no more screaming, just regular breathing in and out. His intense struggle was over; he was going to live.

God works in spectacular ways. He has the view of the world and can arrange the circumstances of His willing servants, to intersect with those who need His help. We thank God for a mission trip, a dedicated volunteer doctor, the gift of free partnership with the Adventist Medical Center, and its remarkable staff.

And we especially thank God for a healthy, bouncing baby boy.

25

What Do I Do with All This Bread?

The food pantry was a bustling place. Over the years, it had grown into a robust part of the agency, serving over 85,000 people every year with food as one of the largest free food distribution centers in the state of Oregon. During those years, it was not unusual for one in five adults to be hungry in Oregon; the figure was even worse for children (one in four). Welfare laws had changed, and more families were finding it increasingly difficult to meet their basic needs.

This increased need pressed the agency to gather more free food from local stores, ask for more donations of food from individuals, and apply for grants to help purchase food at very low rates from the Oregon Food Bank. We felt blessed that the local bakeries always baked abundantly, and grocery stores would share their leftover bread with us. Bread was a basic staple for our clients no matter what nationality they represented or language they spoke.

Asking the Lord to give us more food was not unusual. But to ask the Lord to bring us more bread had never happened. If there was one thing the grocery stores had in abundance, it was bread.

Every day the truck brought in boxes of bread products from the local stores.

But that all changed in a blink of an eye as a surprising side effect of the attack on the Twin Towers in New York City. The economy became tight, and for nearly a year after the attack, the bakeries in town responded to the recession by baking less bread. This saved the bakeries money, but it crippled our ability to provide enough for our clients. Gradually our bread supplies were reduced until one day the shelves were empty. Never before had we run out of bread. Bread was the major topic at our daily worship service that morning. We begged God to somehow supply our great need, and then we went to work as usual. We opened the doors of the pantry, and people came through to get their food. Some asked for bread, but we had to tell them there was none.

About an hour later, a stranger knocked at the back door. He looked bewildered. "Can you use some bread?" he asked. "I just got a whole pickup load of bread from a store. They asked me if I wanted it and I said yes, but I don't really know what I'm going to do with it. I was just driving down the street to figure out where to take it and decided to turn in here." He glanced around. "What is this place? What do you do here?"

"Come in, and we'll show you," was the answer. After touring the bustling pantry, seeing the people carrying groceries out to their cars, and observing the empty bread shelves, his puzzlement turned to amazement. "Well, I'm certain now that you can you use this!" he exclaimed happily, waving toward his heavily laden truck.

The pickup was heaped high with bread, rolls, hot dog buns, tortillas, and burger buns, all of which the store had given to him before we'd even prayed. The Lord answered in our extremity, waiting for a time when we couldn't help ourselves to show us our only hope is to lean on Him. It seems He always answered miraculously when we were being stretched beyond our capabilities while helping His children.

26

CHAPTER

Felts, Anyone?

If you attended Bible classes as a child, you may remember your teacher using colorful felt cutouts of people, animals, trees, rainbows, Noah's ark, and many other pieces to illustrate the Bible story for that day. Your teacher probably told the stories while she carefully patted and rubbed a felt person, cloud, bush, or lion onto a board covered with light blue felt. Gradually, as the felt cutouts stuck to the board, a complete picture was built to illustrate the story. It is safe to say these felt cutouts have been mass-produced for at least the last seven decades. These colorful cutouts were usually affectionately referred to as felts and have become the foundation of nearly every children's Bible teaching arsenal. These teaching aids help the Bible stories come alive, helping children embrace and remember biblical facts and concepts.

There is only one problem with these amazing felts. They come stamped on large sheets of felt, making it necessary for each Bible teacher to spend hours carefully and painstakingly cutting them out. Teachers can now buy them on large sheets of felt, or they can pay a bit more and buy them precut. Either way, purchasing felts is an expensive investment in biblical educational materials.

One day a woman donated a set of felts to PACS. This was the largest set a person could buy, comprised of all the smaller sets available at the time. She was no longer involved in teaching children and fully understood the value of her gift. It was an amazing donation with her only requirement being that the felts could not be sold. The set could be broken up into the smaller subsets if necessary, but nothing could be put for sale in our thrift shop.

This was a most unusual gift, and the PACS staff discussed how it should be handled in order to honor the woman's request and get the felts to whoever could use them. It was suggested that PACS keep the set and use the felts in Bible teaching classes held right at the agency, especially during the summer when vacation Bible school could be offered in the current meeting room. We settled on this plan, and the discussion turned to the felts themselves. Each one of the hundreds of characters, rocks, trees, stars, moons, and pieces must be cut out before they could be used to tell Bible stories. What a job. The exhausted staff was simply too busy to take on this task. It was clear we would not be holding vacation Bible school anytime soon.

Finally, Grace, our always optimistic, energetic health clinic coordinator, offered to take the complete set of felts home and enlist her family's help with the huge project of cutting them out. That night she loaded the felts into the trunk of her car and took them home to her unsuspecting family. They methodically and systematically tackled the job.

Two years later, Grace returned with the felts finished. By that time, things had changed at PACS, and it was obvious we weren't going to be able to hold vacation Bible schools in our meeting room. Through church connections across the city, we began to explore who needed the felts. No one seemed to be able to use the entire set, so we split it into the various subsets for local churches who needed them, also sending some of the subsets overseas as needs were presented. One subset of the felts was left. Months passed. We begged and pleaded, but try as we might, we couldn't get rid of that last set.

Once again, Grace came to the rescue. She had a great crew of volunteer primary care doctors who rotated in and out of the clinic to see patients, with each physician coming for one or more days each month. These physicians were notable for their compassion both in their home city and around the world. When Grace discovered one of the volunteer doctors was going to India for a missionary journey, she asked him to add the last felt subset to the other items he had already packed, to distribute to the local people. It was very hard to say no to Grace, so the doctor reluctantly agreed.

When the doctor's group arrived in India, they dispersed the treasures they'd brought with them to the locals. The days passed until it was almost time to leave. Everything was given out except the felts. No one seemed to want them, but the doctor was determined he would not go back home with those felts in his suitcase. A group of locals gathered on the day he left to thank the doctor's group for their work in India. He impulsively handed the felts to the wife of a Baptist Indian couple who worked in the outlying areas. He asked the couple to give the felts to whoever might be able to use them. When the wife realized what had been thrust into her hands, she burst into tears. The doctor thought perhaps he had made a cultural faux pas of some sort and rushed to apologize. She waived him aside, explaining she had been praying for that exact subset of felts for eight years. God had answered her persistent prayers. For eight years, the Lord had been orchestrating events so that finally this woman's prayer was answered.

How privileged Grace and the doctor felt to be part of God's answer to this woman.

Do you ever pray a long time for something? God is listening, and He hears. You might be amazed at His creative resourcefulness when He answers.

God may also gift you with the opportunity to help answer someone else's prayer. If so, you will be blessed with an amazing, humbling, awesome experience!

27

God Planned It

Tousled, brown-haired Danny was by nature a bright and inquisitive boy. A busy nine-year-old, his insatiable curiosity and abundant imagination often teamed together to make him mischievous and creative. On top of that, Danny was a smart kid, loved school, and made excellent grades. His friendly nature and happy disposition endeared him to kids and teachers alike.

But tonight was different. Danny was scared. He held his mother's hand tightly and looked down at the carpet as they walked together into the health clinic. He was very quiet, and his normally dancing brown eyes were sad, even a little worried. The clinic was open into the evening on this day, so his mother had been able to get him an appointment after school hours.

Danny and his mother were ushered into an exam room. The doctor entered, and with him came another doctor. The clinic doctor explained, "This is my friend. He wanted to shadow me because he's heard about the clinic and wanted to visit it tonight. Is that all right?"

Danny's mother agreed. Her eyes were anxious, and she spoke quickly to the doctor. "Danny's teacher referred us to this clinic.

She's concerned that Danny may not hear well." His mother glanced at Danny, "Danny is usually a good boy, but lately he's been ignoring instructions. He blows off the teachers and acts like they don't exist. He's getting into trouble because he ignores them, and sometimes stays late on the playground, choosing to disregard the bell calling everyone inside."

"How are his grades?" asked the doctor.

Danny's mother continued, "He used to get good grades, but now he is failing in every subject. Sometimes he even ignores me when I try to talk to him. He says he didn't hear me, but I'm not always sure. He's basically a good boy, so that's why the teacher sent us here."

Danny glanced up at the doctor.

"Hop up here, sonny," the doctor said as he patted the exam table. "Let me take a look." Danny quickly jumped up on the table. The doctor looked in each ear. "Well," he said thoughtfully, "the teachers might be right. Danny seems to have some difficulties in his ears, but it's nothing we can't fix. He will do much better with a tube put in each ear."

"Oh, dear," his mother exclaimed at this news. "I injured myself a few months ago, so I have not been able to work. I've lost my health insurance. There is no way I could pay for a procedure like that. Isn't there something else you could do that would fix his ears? I couldn't possibly afford ear tubes."

At that, the visiting doctor interrupted the mom. "May I take a look at his ears?" Danny's mother agreed. "Here, young man," the doctor said. "Let me take a look. Yes, yes, hmm." He carefully examined each ear. Finally, he stood up and turned to Danny's mother. "What the clinic doctor tells you is true. Danny does need ear tubes. In fact, he needs them quickly. Now, I want you to listen carefully to me. It just happens that I am an ear specialist. I treat boys like Danny all the time. With ear tubes, his misbehaving and bad grades will go away. Without them, Danny will continue to struggle, and lasting damage could occur. I just happened to visit the clinic this evening to observe, but your son needs this procedure, and I can provide it."

"But I can't pay you," Danny's mother cried. "Maybe Danny will get better on his own?"

The doctor replied, "I know you can't pay me, but I'd be honored if you would let me do this for Danny without charging anything. I will make all the arrangements with my office. They will call you and set up an appointment. He will get excellent care, and I will want to see him again in my office for follow-up after we've done the procedure."

God's special timing brought all the right people together, at the right time, and with the right skills. Danny's mother was ecstatic with joy and relief. She couldn't believe someone would be so kind. Danny became the bright, precocious, smart, and lovable boy he had been before. His grades came back up, he came in from recess on time, and his teachers were proud of him. But he still indulged in a bit of mischief every once in a while.

28

CHAPTER

Hope Is Made for Sharing

Charlene was distraught as she got off the bus in front of PACS early one Sunday afternoon. She blinked in the bright sunshine, briefly noticing that it was going to be hot that day. After furtively glancing about her, she darted across the asphalt parking spaces to the glass door of the thrift store, pushed against it, and bolted in.

Customers browsed quietly through the racks of clothes, shoes, and linens. Music played softly overhead, but Charlene noticed none of that. She ran straight to the cash register, which was conveniently placed right near the entrance. The thrift shop manager was tending to some items placed around the cash register and looked up in surprise.

"Please, help me!" Charlene implored hysterically. Charlene was frightened, and her face was bruised. She was a short, tiny woman in her early forties. Her long blonde hair hung below her shoulders, with bangs coming over her eyes. She obviously felt in danger, and her eyes darted back to the door, fully expecting to see someone following her. She couldn't feel safe here, especially because the front wall of the thrift shop was floor-to-ceiling windows.

The manager ushered Charlene back through double doors and into the area where food was donated. This was the weekend, so the food area was empty, and it was in the back of the building, providing some privacy. There were no windows in the food area, and all the doors were locked. Furthermore, the thrift store manager knew another volunteer, Nancy, had come in to work in the back. With a brief introduction, the manager left Charlene and Nancy to return to the customers browsing in the thrift shop.

Nancy, a middle-aged woman with prematurely beautiful silver hair, was a hard and faithful worker. She came to PACS every weekday to help coordinate food deliveries, sort commodities, and stock shelves in the food pantry. On weekdays, the food pantry was crowded and teeming with activity—people coming and going, the forklift moving pallets, and freezers and refrigerators constantly being refilled. It was normal to give out over a ton of food every day to up to one hundred hungry individuals and families. Nancy rarely had the opportunity to visit extensively with people who came for food. She often came in on Sundays, which was usually a quiet time to restock, but God seemed to have another plan for her that day.

Nancy stopped her work and sat down to visit with Charlene. Charlene slowly revealed her story. She had lived in an abusive situation for three years. She'd left once but felt forced to return.

The night before, her husband beat her again, all the while threatening to kill her. It was the worst beating yet; she truly believed she might die. In the morning, after he left, she dragged herself, sore and bruised, to the bus stop. Shortly, the bus appeared and opened its doors, and she boarded, glad to get away. After collapsing into an empty seat, exhausted, she looked around to get her bearings. Oh, no! There he was! Her husband sat just a few seats away.

Suddenly he jumped up and rushed at her, yelling obscenities and threatening her. The bus driver stopped the bus and managed to intervene long enough for Charlene to stumble down the aisle and out the door, leaving her husband still on the bus—right in front of PACS. The bus driver quickly drove away before her husband could follow her.

Charlene continued her story. Her Christian grandmother had raised her, but the principles of self-worth and her inherent value in God's eyes had not meant much to her as a child. Still, her grandmother's love instilled a sense of dignity and a desire to survive. Now God had led her to a place of help. For two hours, she sobbed out her dilemma. Nancy had no long-term solutions for her but sensed that she simply needed to be available to listen. She asked a few questions that might help her decide what to do. Charlene's story tore at her heart, and Nancy felt overwhelmed. She prayed for the patience and strength to continue listening.

Charlene eventually calmed down and talked herself into the certainty of leaving the dangerous situation where she lived. She remembered her Christian grandmother and garnered strength from her upbringing, connecting the instructions from childhood with the hope and the prayer that Nancy offered. Nancy was able to help her find a shelter for women fleeing abusive situations. When a shelter worker came to take Charlene to the safe house, Charlene was composed and resolute.

Upon reflection, Nancy saw God's handiwork in the experience, saying, "I really didn't do much but offer her some hope. And it wasn't the hope I offered her that made the difference. I don't think you can put hope in a little box and send someone away with it. The seed of self-worth was planted by God through her grandmother, and in time it would become Charlene's hope and reality. God used my words to underscore the message of love, which He had been telling Charlene all her life."

Did Charlene stick to her decision to leave her husband permanently? We never found out. What we do know is in her despair, God guided her, and she unknowingly stumbled upon PACS for sanctuary. Nancy was there to listen. Charlene shared her deepest despair. She sensed the message "You matter," and it comforted her. Through that human connection, she found hope and power.

29

CHAPTER

Averting Abortion

The shrill ring of my black desk phone startled me from my intense concentration on a grant-writing project. It was nearing 8:30 at night; if I stayed focused, I could finish in another hour. Constant interruptions throughout the day demanded that I wait to concentrate on writing, after we had closed the doors for the day. Staff and volunteers had stopped by my open door, cheerily saying goodbye and warning me not to stay too long. Even the jovial, deaf janitor had come and gone with much smiling and gesturing, struggling to communicate to me through sign language that he and his wife were doing well and happy to be working at PACS.

The phone rang again. I glanced out the window, even though by now it was too dark to see whether the wind and rain had increased, as was predicted earlier in the day. I didn't want to answer the insistent ringing; it was way beyond closing time, and I needed to get this finished. Only someone I knew would know to find me here this time of day. I glanced at the phone to see the number displayed over the keys and didn't recognize it. *How did someone I don't know get my private extension? Should I answer?*

The phone rang insistently. With resignation, I wiped my hand down my weary face, pushed my hair back, and picked up the receiver. "Hello?" I said simply, wearily dispensing with the usual mouthful, but more pleasant greeting of "Portland Adventist Community Services. How may I help you?"

"What's the address of the nearest abortion clinic? My wife needs one now," a man loudly demanded in broken English.

Instantly alert, I held the phone away from my ear, questions whizzing through my mind. *Was she injured? Had he discovered the baby was not his? Why was he so distraught?*

"Can you tell me why she needs an abortion?" I asked gently, trying to calm him down. "What is causing this emergency?"

The man responded by telling me a story. "This is not the first time she has been pregnant. She got pregnant before and had some problems. We couldn't afford to take her to a doctor, and we knew something was wrong, so we took her to an abortion clinic and had the baby aborted. Now she's pregnant again, and the same thing is happening. We came to your clinic today because it is free, and they sent us to get an ultrasound to find out the problem. But we can't pay for that test." By now he was sobbing. I had difficulty understanding him, and his increased distress made it even harder. "We want to keep this baby, but we can't. We have no other choice. We must get an abortion tonight." I could hear his wife wailing with grief in the background.

Praying for guidance, I responded, "Please don't do anything right now. I will make a couple phone calls for you. I will check to see if there is anything I can do to help you."

"No, there is nothing that can be done," he responded. "We've done everything we can. Just give me the number of the abortion clinic."

I pleaded politely but authoritatively, "Please, sir. I'll call you back in fifteen minutes with an answer. Will you wait that long for me?" He hesitated, so I continued pressing. "Only fifteen minutes is all I'm asking. Please don't do anything until I call you back." Finally, he agreed.

While continuing to pray silently, I called our clinic manager, Julie. She remembered the couple. They were so excited about this baby but were worried that things might be going wrong with the pregnancy. The doctor who'd examined her did not think the pregnancy was in trouble, but just to be sure, he had referred her to a place that would provide the ultrasound at no cost. The appointment was scheduled for the next day. Evidently, the couple had not understood the test was completely free for them and their baby.

Within the allotted fifteen minutes, I called him back. I explained the ultrasound was free. He was silent, trying to absorb this new information. He asked me to explain it to him again. "This test is completely free for you. You will not have to pay anything," I repeated. "Your appointment is tomorrow morning. They will be able to tell whether your baby is having problems. Please let your wife have the scan before you decide she must have an abortion. Please, just sleep tonight and take her in tomorrow morning." After a very long conversation, he finally agreed. Relieved and concerned, I hung up the phone, feeling like God had kept me there late so I could answer this couple's frantic call. With renewed energy, I finished up my grant writing, stepped out into the howling wind and driving rain, and went home for the night.

The next day, I didn't hear anything—or the next, or the next. Finally, bursting with curiosity, I checked with Julie, our health clinic manager. What had happened? Had they gotten the test? She told me the couple had followed my request and gone to get the ultrasound at their scheduled appointment. Yes, it confirmed their baby was fine, there was no problem, and they could expect a normal delivery. They were ecstatic with joy. They could have children and be a family—a dream that had eluded them for many years.

For the next few months, his wife came regularly for checkups and several months later delivered a beautiful, healthy, little girl. They arrived for the first postnatal checkup with their pride and joy, a darling pink bundle of sleeping baby, as well as an armful of roses for the clinic volunteers. Joyous tears of the nurses and doctors mingled with the proud parents as they hugged and congratulated each other. A year later, on the date of her first birthday, the family returned. Again, happy and thankful tears overflowed in praise to a God, who specializes in bringing His children hope and joy amid times of great crisis.

30

CHAPTER

Friendly Frog Fred

H e would have fit comfortably on a quarter. His tiny green body shivered, crouching low on the open palm. He tried unsuccessfully to become invisible, but it wasn't working.

The day began reasonably well for him. His routine went uninterrupted as he hopped about among the plants around the front steps of the house. The person who lived here was an excellent gardener. He had seen her many times digging, planting, and rearranging. She knew just how to make the perfect frog haven, which he was fully enjoying on this warm, sunny morning. He crawled up onto the doorstep to explore something new. It must be something else the gardener had prepared for his pleasure. He'd seen her drive away earlier, so he cautiously crawled into the big, white, new place, finding it deliciously cool and semidark. You and I would have identified it as a refrigerator left on the doorstep with the door slightly ajar. It was the perfect place for a quick little frog nap.

Bang! Suddenly the door closed. Without warning, he was trapped in a strange place in pitch-black darkness. He found himself being thrown about inside the blackness. *Bumpety-bump. Bumpety-bump.* It was moving!

The refrigerator was loaded into a truck and whisked away. Finally, the motion stopped, the door opened, and someone exclaimed, "Oh, look—a frog!" The sudden brightness blinded him; he stayed motionless, hoping he'd be invisible.

But no, the danger came closer. He was scooped up, in the wrong place at the wrong time. People gathered around, peering at him on the open palm. The hand closed around him again in preparation to take him outdoors. As the fingers closed, he heard, "Wait, let me take him home." One of the volunteers, afraid the frog would not survive in this new neighborhood, rescued him. The volunteer dubbed him Fred and then prepared an elaborate new frog home for him stocked with an abundance of frog food. He discovered more crickets than he'd ever seen in one place and croaked his delight all night. The well-meaning volunteer quickly discovered having a frog growing up in his bedroom was not conducive to getting a good night's sleep. Fred was growing quickly and becoming even more vocal, especially at night. The volunteer decided to offer Fred to his sister, a third-grade teacher on the Oregon coast.

And so a new life began for Fred. The volunteer's sister made plans to place him in her classroom. She began to write letters, posing as Fred. "I'm coming to join your classroom," Fred wrote through the teacher. "Will you like me?"

Thinking Fred was going to be a new student, they wrote back, "Yes. How many brothers and sisters do you have?"

"Oh, about a hundred, I guess," he replied. The children started wondering. Could this be an animal instead of a new student?

After many letters, Fred arrived. He was immediately loved and tenderly cared for by the entire class. Growing bigger thanks to his steady supply of crickets, Fred hid most of the day in the foliage of his frog home.

He wrote to shy children. He comforted children who were sad. He seemed to know who needed him. Fred was always there, always lending a listening ear, and always writing a word of encouragement. For Fred knew hard times. Fred knew about loneliness. Fred knew about being scared.

We smile at the story of Fred. It is a true story, though some details have been enhanced. But seriously, haven't we all had hard times? Don't you remember being lonely and scared?

Share these memories. You have the qualifications. You can help others, just as Fred was qualified to help the schoolchildren.

Fred's story has a tragic ending because Fred lost his life early one morning when someone robbed the school and then set it on fire. The loss of Fred was devastating to the teacher and children alike. They grieved his death because they had lost a friend, not a mere frog.

The story of Fred can be helpful for decades to come. If we can remember Fred's example and how he enriched the lives of others, his life will have accomplished its God-directed mission.

God gave each of us a gift in Fred, that tiny little bit of green with the big, frightened eyes. We thank Him for reminding us that each of us has a God-given individual mission for God. Even if we're frightened, the Lord will use us wherever we find ourselves.

31

CHAPTER

Unanswered Questions

Elaine carried herself with aloof dignity, her hair pulled back to the nape of her neck in a thick mass of wavy brown locks. She almost glided into the waiting room. She was keenly aware of how differently she was dressed than others who were waiting. They were casually dressed in T-shirts, jeans, and tennis shoes, whereas she wore navy slacks, a crisp white cotton blouse and navy-blue loafers.

When people needed to come for food or other items, it was customary to have them wait in a waiting room until it was their turn to visit with an interviewer. The interviewers were volunteers; most of them had their own stories of bad times when they needed help. Many of them, even though now they were interviewers, still qualified for food and medical care through the agency. Sometimes they almost acted as lay counselors in their interactions with people who often had both temporal and spiritual needs.

It wasn't long until Ellen was invited into a small room that had one desk, a computer, and two chairs. The interviewer greeted her warmly, "Good morning, Ellen. Please have a seat. How can we help you today?"

"This is very difficult for me," Ellen commented softly, carrying herself almost elegantly as she walked into the interview room and sank into one of the chairs. "I have always been the one helping people, and now I have to ask for help." Grateful for a private place and sympathizing ear, Ellen began to cry.

The interviewer gently handed her some tissue and then began to assess her needs. Yes, she needed food. No, she didn't need anything else. What else might be helpful to her?

At this question, Ellen began to sob uncontrollably. "Please pray for me." Her sobs made her hard to understand. She collected herself a bit and apologized profusely for her loss of control in front of the interviewer. Then she explained, "Three years ago, I was diagnosed with terminal cancer. It's been a long journey. I've had seven surgeries, and right now I'm doing a little better. I had to quit work because of all the medical issues, so I lost my medical insurance, and now I'm on disability." Her voice broke, but she continued. "My first husband divorced me, and I have our fourteen-year-old son, who has been the rock of my life these last three years. But now my ex has decided to default on child support. My son is too young to work, and my disability is not enough for the two of us. Please pray that something may change for our situation."

The counselor began to pray but was suddenly interrupted. "I have not told you everything," Ellen cried. "Please pray for my daughter too. I didn't tell you I had a second marriage with someone of a different nationality. That marriage didn't go well, and when he saw we were headed for divorce, he kidnapped our daughter and fled back to his old country. She is six years old, and I'm not allowed to talk to her or have any communication. My life is a nightmare. I have so many questions, especially now that I may not live very long."

The questions haunted Ellen. Where was her daughter? Would she ever see her again? Would she ever be able to hold her sweet little girl in her arms again? Would her daughter ever know what happened to her mother? And who would take care of her son when he no longer had a mother? How would he survive? Would he stay out of trouble? Who would he marry? Would he have children of his own? Would his life be better than hers?

She asked all those questions in the little interview room that day. There were no answers, but there was a listening ear and a referral for an appropriate case manager. Finally, she composed herself, looked up with a calm smile, and declared, "In spite of all that's happened to us, God has been good." With that affirmation, Ellen gathered her food, held her head high and serenely walked into the sunshine to embrace another day.

32

CHAPTER

Post-Surgery Woes

The health clinic was literally a lifesaver for many people with no medical insurance. The doctors and nurses in the clinic were all volunteers, donating huge amounts of time to keep the clinic open. Over the course of a year, it was not unusual for them to treat more than a thousand patients. Funding for the clinic came from churches, individuals, and foundations while working in conjunction with the Multnomah County Health Department.

For many years, the clinic partnered with a local foundation and the state health system to provide free annual breast and cervical exams. Many women who otherwise would never have seen a doctor were able to get care. Occasionally, something suspicious was detected, and the patient was referred to Portland Adventist Medical Center (PAMC) or Oregon Health Sciences University (OHSU) for further testing and possibly surgery. Then the patient would return to the health clinic for postsurgery follow up. Every part of this care, even surgery, was free to the patient.

Peggy was a patient who had originally come to PACS for a free breast exam and mammogram. Because of findings from the exam and the mammogram, Peggy was designated a candidate for surgery, chemotherapy, and radiation. She cooperated with her treatment protocols, which took several months to complete. The doctors and nurses helped her navigate the confusing world of multiple doctors' appointments and coping with the many side effects of the treatments.

Nearly a year after her initial appointment, the day came for her last visit to the clinic. She was doing well, the treatments were finished, and her follow-up tests were all negative. The staff was excited about her progress, but she was not happy. She endured the visit but was glum and despondent.

Concerned, the doctor and nurses asked her many questions, trying to find out the reason for her sadness. Peggy managed to avoid most of the questions, but an unbidden stray tear slid down Peggy's cheek, making way for another and another. The doctor listened as Peggy poured out her heart. The cancer had been invasive, making it necessary to remove one complete breast. This was devastating to Peggy.

"I just don't feel like a woman anymore. I try to dress so it won't be noticed, but it's so obvious. I know that everyone who looks at me can tell I'm only partly there. I barely have enough money to pay my rent and buy the medicine I need, much less afford a prosthesis." Peggy finished by wailing, "I wish I'd never had the surgery."

Sadly, the staff acknowledged her sentiments. She was right: breast prostheses were expensive, and they must be fit to each person individually. No two prostheses were alike. Each one must be exactly the right size and the right shape, and like a shoe, a prosthesis must fit the right side. And yet if Peggy felt like she looked good, she would be able to find a new meaning to life.

Then the clinic manager remembered something. "Wait a minute," she said. She went to a cupboard in the back room. After finding a stool, she reached up to the far left of the top shelf. Stretching high to reach clear to the very back, she pulled out a brown paper bag. She handed it to Peggy, saying, "Nine months ago, someone donated this prosthesis and garment. When I saw it,

I thought, *Who would want this?* and put it up out of the way. Why don't you try it on?"

The staff waited anxiously. Would it be the correct size, fit, and shape? Would God have provided just the right prosthesis?

At last, Peggy emerged from the exam room beaming radiantly. It was a perfect fit and she looked wonderful. With hugs, tears, and high-fives all around, the staff celebrated the beginning of a new life for Peggy. Peggy was no longer glum and depressed; now she couldn't stop smiling and laughing. Her depression was gone. Not only had God brought her physical healing, but He had also satisfied the deepest desire of her heart.

33

CHAPTER

Turn Up the Music

The day was typical for Portland, or at least typical for how most people imagine the northwest United States. An insistent drizzle fell from the gray clouds overhead. It was almost like heavy fog, not really raining but enough to make everything drippy and damp. If you had to be outside, you needed a coat and waterproof shoes, but rarely would you need an umbrella. People ventured outside reluctantly on those days, especially in the early autumn, hoping for a drier day to dawn before heading out for serious shopping in the big city.

However, businesses did not look at the sky to decide whether to open their doors for customers. Despite the dreary day, PACS was bustling and busy as usual.

But it was not busy in the gift shop. Cindy, the one and only gift shop cashier, was having a slow day. Cindy loved her little post, as she dubbed her spot in the gift shop. It was like a quiet sanctuary for her. All the items in the gift shop were brand-new. Thanks to the talents and hours of work donated by the gift shop committee, the candles and crèmes were beautifully displayed, scenting the air with vanilla, apple, and pumpkin spice. The children's corner boasted pink, yellow, blue, and lavender baby items; quilts, bath sets, games, puzzles, and toys. The card rack burst with colorful greeting, birthday, sympathy, and get-well cards, and alongside was a whimsical display of birds, cats, and frogs. In contrast, in a lighted glass display case were expensive watches, clocks, and elegant glass figurines. Opposite the glass display case and over on the dark forest-green slat wall, larger clocks hung, chimed on the hour, had moving pieces, and played songs. The atmosphere in the shop celebrated the season, with decorations of pumpkins, tiny hay bales, little outhouses with moons on them, and golden shocks of corn. Soft Christian music always played in the background, an advertisement that there were lovely CDs of hymns available for sale. Three walls of the shop were waist-to-ceiling glass windows, creating an open, bright feeling even on dreary days such as this.

Cindy had some paperwork to do because she kept track of the data needed for reports to the governing board and to the Oregon Food Bank. Even so, she liked it when people sauntered in and looked around at all the pretty things. She liked it even better when someone would buy something, especially something expensive, like one of the clocks on the wall. Whenever she had an especially good sale, Cindy waited until the customer left, and then she quickly locked the door, ran into my office, and told me all about it. She was so excited and would describe customers in detail, noting exactly what they'd bought and how nice they were. We would rejoice together because her excitement was contagious.

But today, it seemed few people were interested in buying anything. People came in the shop, looked around, and left. A couple of people bought chocolate bars, which Cindy kept by the cash register. Cindy was bored and a little restless. She gazed out the windows at the rain for a while, reflecting and praying over the names of customers whom she had promised to bring to God daily. She loved to pray; it was one of her special gifts, which she offered to anyone willing to accept. Many of her regular customers came and bought things, but they really came to be blessed by Cindy's special gift of encouragement and support. While perched on her high padded chair, she stirred from her reverie, idly bent down, and changed the music to keep herself occupied.

After a while, a young lady sauntered through the door. She wandered up and down the aisles, looking at things but not seeming to have a purpose. Maybe she was simply avoiding the drippy weather outside. Somehow, Cindy felt impressed to turn up the music. She felt it strange to turn the music louder, so she sat quietly and didn't change the volume. The lady continued to pick things up, examine them, and set them down, lost in the world of her own thoughts. Again Cindy felt impressed, this time a little more urgently: *Turn up the music.*

A little perplexed, Cindy obeyed the thought in her head and turned up the volume. The beautiful hymns filled the gift shop. In a few minutes the young lady asked, "What is that music you're playing?" As Cindy showed it to her, she exclaimed, "That's just lovely. Can I buy it?"

Then the story tumbled out. The young lady was distraught, aimlessly wandering, taking a break, and trying to cope. Her mother was home, dying of cancer. The mother struggled with the thought of dying, what would happen to her, and what would happen to her daughter; her pain was both physical and emotional. The young lady had tried and tried, but nothing she said comforted her mother. She was exhausted from the effort and felt excruciating agony when she observed her mother's grief. The young lady's heart was touched and comforted by the gorgeous hymns filling the gift shop, and she instinctively knew the music would help her mother find peace as well.

When telling this story, Cindy always gives God the credit for impressing her to turn up the music. Because Cindy responded to her impressions, she was able to visit with this young woman. She was able to talk with her, provide her with something to comfort her mother, and invite her back. Cindy learned that making a sale is nice and even necessary, but making a friend is paramount.

34

CHAPTER

Bunk Beds for Little Boys

The day was finished. All the customers had left the thrift store, the volunteers had gone home, and Jim, the thrift ministry manager, removed his keys from the lock in the door. He turned to count the cash register money, satisfied that another good day was finished.

Suddenly someone banged on the door. Startled, Jim turned around and came back. Jim began to explain through the locked door that the store was closed for the day and to please come back tomorrow.

The man would have none of it. Through broken English and many gestures, the man managed to communicate to Jim that he was desperate to come in. Finally, Jim opened the door so they could talk face-to-face.

"I see you have bunk beds for sale," the man began. "I really need those beds for my sons." He nodded proudly toward the boys, who were gazing solemnly at this exchange. Jim guessed the dark-haired, brown-eyed boys were probably about six and eight years old.

"I've been saving as fast as I could, and today I got paid, so now I finally have enough money to buy the beds you have displayed in the window. I work very hard and many hours," the man proudly continued. "I took off work early so I could make it here before you closed. You know what traffic's like in Portland at five o'clock in the evening. I hurried as quickly as I could, but I'm too late. You are closed. I don't know when I'll be able to get off work early again." He was visibly upset, his hands clasped to his head while he ran his fingers through his thick, dark hair. "Please, sir," he pleaded. "My sons are sleeping on the floor. Won't you please sell the beds to me even though you are closed?"

Jim listened carefully to the man. Although the man didn't know it, Jim would soon be finished with his work for the day and go home to his own children. His thoughts went to his children, not that different in ages than these boys. His kids had their own beds. He couldn't imagine children with no bed to sleep in, much less to bounce and tumble and play on. Jim was a compassionate individual, and the man didn't really need to plead with him. Jim's heart was already in tune with the man's plight.

"Of course," exclaimed Jim cheerfully. "I'll be more than happy to sell you the beds." With that, he took the man's hard-earned money, reopened the cash register, and gave him a receipt. Then Jim helped the man take the beds apart and load the pieces in his pickup. The boys, awestruck at first, got more excited at the prospect of having their own beds, running and tumbling around the two men until their father had to tell them to settle down and behave.

"Oh, thank you, thank you," the man kept repeating. "Some people just expect to be given everything without ever paying for things. What's the word for that in English? Charity? Yes, charity." He went on. "I work hard. I work many hours at more than one job. I don't earn very much, but I save and go to stores like this one, where I can get things for my family without having to ask for free things. Come on, boys, get in," he commanded as they ran past Jim one last time.

"Charity, charity." He nearly spat the words out of his mouth, talking to no one in particular. Then he turned to Jim and said simply, "You make me and my family very happy tonight. Thank you. Good night, sir."

With that, Jim locked the thrift shop doors, finished counting the money for the day, and went home to his family. Remembering the two little boys who now had their own beds, Jim gave each of his own children an extra special hug as he tucked them into bed that night.

35

CHAPTER

A Final Wish

The stuffed animal donated that day was huge. It was a full five feet tall. It was a big, fluffy, soft animal. In fact, it was a bright yellow, fluffy, soft, stuffed animal. It had an oversized head with two big blue eyes and very long black eyelashes. It had a rather narrow chest with a round tummy and looked best when it was sitting with its brown feet thrust out in front of it. It was meant to cuddle and be cuddled.

Everyone recognized him immediately: it was the famous Tweety Bird from the *Looney Tunes* cartoons produced by the Warner Brothers Studios. Historically, Tweety, a fictional baby yellow canary, has had a long life, first being introduced in the 1940s and reappearing at different times even as late as 2010. All of us knew the tiny, fictional, lovable Tweety Bird. We thought he had never looked so magnificent as when he came to us as a huge, soft, fuzzy, stuffed animal.

We were excited. Tweety was priced high because we wanted someone to buy him who could afford to pay a lot and thus support our agency. We felt people who could afford twenty-five dollars on a huge stuffed animal didn't need food or clothing, and in those days the twenty-five dollars would help us buy enough food to feed a family of four for a month. Tweety Bird was placed high on an overhead shelf in the thrift store. He was admired by customers and volunteers alike, but he was too expensive; it would take just the right person to have the money to afford him.

About a week later, a man came up to me, pointed to the overhead shelf in the store, and said, "Could I have that Tweety Bird?"

"Sure," I replied, glancing at him quickly and reaching for Tweety's price tag.

"No, no, you don't understand," he protested. "I don't want to buy him. I just want you to give him to me." Now he was demanding.

Not everyone who came to our agency had the best of intentions. This man fit my stereotypical image of someone who lived hard and fast. I was aware of how often things were given out of our store to people we thought were deserving, and then the items were sold for drug money. "Why should I give him to you?" I asked warily.

He replied, "Because I know a little boy who's sick, and he would like Tweety Bird. That's what he really wants."

I thought, *Oh, sure, likely story. Now I've heard it all. Another person takes advantage of me. From all outward appearances, this man has a long history of addiction.* I was disappointed that we might lose out on a good sale for the store. But for some reason, I let him have the huge stuffed animal. I don't know why; it wasn't a mark of great compassion. I somehow felt I should let him have Tweety Bird. He took the bird and disappeared out the door. I completely forgot about the whole incident.

A few weeks later, as I was walking through the store, a man came up to me and asked, "Do you remember me?"

I looked at him quizzically, suddenly recognized him, and thought, *Yeah, I remember you. What do you want this time?* The last image I remembered was of him carrying a free Tweety Bird under his arm, the bright yellow prize of the thrift shop, and disappearing out the door, never looking back.

"Do you remember Tweety Bird?" he asked quietly.

"Yes," I relied. "What happened to him?"

I learned that Tweety Bird went out our doors, traveled all the way across Portland (including crossing the river that goes through downtown Portland), and climbed the hill to Oregon Health Sciences University, a medical facility that included a children's hospital. Tweety was whisked through the hospital doors, down the hall, up the elevator, down more halls, and past the nurses' desk. Then he was perched on a chair right inside the door of little Joey's room as he lay soundly sleeping.

Joey, just five years old, was very tiny, and very ill. His hair was gone, exposing his bald head. He didn't eat much anymore, and an intravenous pole was his constant companion. He had begged his dad to let him see Tweety Bird. It was his one and only wish.

When Joey awoke, his eyes immediately focused on the chair by his door. He couldn't believe it. Tweety Bird had come! He was so excited that he insisted the huge bird be placed in bed beside him. He tired quickly, lay back in his bed, and hugged and hugged Tweety, telling the bird over and over how much he had longed for him and how he loved him.

Day and night, Joey lay with his arms around the big, fluffy, stuffed animal. Tweety sat by him in his bed when Joey ate or watched TV. Tweety slept with Joey every night, always there whenever Joey needed him. Joey never let Tweety out of his sight.

"Yes," Joey's dad told me, "Joey loved Tweety. Thank you for letting me take Tweety to him. Tweety brought peace to my tiny little boy." I was shocked as I heard him say, "Joey died of cancer just two weeks ago." After five long, excruciating days, Joey closed his eyes for the last time, still hugging his beloved Tweety Bird, the only thing he had wished for during his lengthy and lingering illness.

I never saw Joey's dad or Tweety again, but I know without a doubt that God was looking after both with love beyond measure. Tweety had a special purpose, and I imagine Tweety continued to have a special purpose wherever he may have gone. Thank you, Lord, for so lavishly granting the very last wish of a tiny, dying boy in a great, big hospital.

36

CHAPTER

Life Is a Trip! Live It Up!

The tabloid, placed provocatively in the supermarket checkout line, screamed at me. I blinked at it absently, and then the import of the words grabbed my attention. I took a closer look. "Life is a trip! Live it up!" I pondered, *If life is a trip, where are we going? Where is the beginning? Where is the end? When do we start, and when do we end? And if it truly is a trip, how many are following the advice to live it up?*

My thoughts turned to Lucy. Lucy planned to work until her greatly anticipated new baby was born. But then, to Lucy and her husband's joy and amazement, they discovered their baby was going to be twins. The doctors warned that Lucy's was a high-risk pregnancy. Sure enough, in the fourth month, she had to quit work in favor of complete bed rest for her growing twins. She carried them until almost full term. Then, tragically and unexpectedly, despite heroic efforts by their expert medical team, the twins were stillborn. Since then, her world had been turned upside down. She had not been able to return to work in a timely manner due to her grief over their loss. Her husband, also devastated, had turned to alcohol and could no longer hold a job. They were now without any income and needed help with food and clothing for themselves and their two-year-old. As she sobbed out her story, she asked for special prayer that her life might get better.

Yes, Lucy and her husband were on a life trip, but not a trip they would choose.

Next, Ed came to mind. His life had taken an unexpected turn. The job that had supported him and his family for years had suddenly evaporated, and he couldn't find another job. Ed had applied for jobs everywhere he could think of, but he rarely got a return reply or scored even an introductory interview. The economy was depressed, jobs were few, and the number of job applicants was astronomical. Days turned into weeks and weeks turned into months, and now the savings Ed had carefully accrued were almost depleted. Next week, he and his family would be evicted from the house they had mortgaged. He was frantic to find a place for them. We were able to help him find a place for Ed and his family while connecting him to additional resources to help in his emergency, and then we sent him home with groceries to help him save the little money left in his wallet.

Ed was also on a life trip, but not the life trip he'd expected.

And what about Larry's life? He didn't feel good. He was tired and listless and had no ambition for anything these days. He heard about PACS's free medical clinic, so he scheduled a routine medical checkup. With no medical insurance, Larry didn't visit the doctor until he was desperate. The doctor discovered Larry's blood pressure was dangerously out of control. With the help of free medication provided through doctor's offices and pharmaceutical programs, weekly visits for checkups, and lifestyle education, Larry gradually grew better. He began to smile and walk with a spring in his step. His family was important to him, and he enjoyed them more and more.

The long bus ride from northeast Portland became an adventure for Larry; he looked forward to visiting with his newfound friends who worked at the clinic. As he improved, his visits became more infrequent, and after a while we rarely saw him.

One sunny morning a couple of years later, Larry appeared at the clinic intake window. He was sad and haggard. The staff was overjoyed to see him again and gathered around him, concerned over his dejected demeanor. With difficulty, he explained that his grandson had committed suicide the night before, and he simply needed someone to talk to about it. He knew he would find a listening ear, a warm hug, and an earnest prayer among his friends in the clinic. When the sun arose that morning, he'd boarded the bus and traveled for nearly two hours among the busy traffic to come to PACS, just to talk. Larry expressed his gratefulness for the care he'd received over the past few years. "I was so sick," Larry told me, "but then I came here. Without PACS, I'd be dead."

How could Larry "live it up" on his life trip?

Yes, I agree with the tabloid. Life is most certainly a trip. It is a unique journey for each person—a journey of many colors, experiences, cares, burdens, joys, and wonders. I'm not sure that any of us have the option to live it up in the way the newspaper was recommending: be adventurous, party day and night, play with your relationships, blow off responsibility, live totally for yourself, and do it now before you die. The reality is that most of us do not have idyllic lives. What's more, living for ourselves soon becomes pointless and shallow. Life can be full of deeper thoughts, loftier goals, and more inclusive ambitions that lead to lasting satisfaction no matter the situations in which we find ourselves.

Although we could not change the circumstances of the lives we touched at PACS, we could add or enhance the more important spiritual component and point them to Jesus. Our goal was to reveal Jesus to everyone who came within our doors. If we could portray the love of Jesus, and if we cared for others as He would, they might learn to trust Him, the only One who can change everything. Only then will life become a trip to be lived—lived through eternity with our very best friend, Jesus. Then we will be totally living it up!

37

CHAPTER ========================

Writing with God

The years passed swiftly at PACS. The economy peaked and dipped. We'd moved to a new location. We'd changed how we served people. We grew not only in the numbers of people we served but in square footage, numbers of vehicles, food picked up, and increased service delivery. Now we were using pallet jacks and a forklift to manage the food we were giving away. We measured things in tons, not pounds. More volunteers kept coming, and more people needed our help. Change was constant, keeping us in a continual state of inadequate help. Reliable staffing was hard to keep; we couldn't maintain competitive wages, and people got burned out because of the heavy workload. Our budget grew, and fundraising became more crucial.

Though we had excellent grant writers over the years, it seemed I also spent most of my time frantically fundraising and writing grants, which was helpful, but most of the grants available would not fund personnel costs. I wondered how foundations expected us to adequately use money designated only for equipment or supplies when we didn't have enough manpower to use the new equipment or hand out the much-needed supplies. In fact, one day when I visited a potential grantor, he told me, "You have too many volunteers. You cannot sustain PACS unless you increase your payroll." True to his word, he gave us a small grant to be used only to support personnel.

One day, I received a grant application allowing us to request a sizable amount of funding for agency operation, including some for payroll. If we could qualify, receiving this grant would give us enough money so I could relax on operational fundraising long enough to focus on stabilizing our staffing. This was crucial at this stage of our business growth. The problem was I didn't discover the grant until the application was due the next day. It normally took many weeks to assemble the data and documentation needed to apply for a grant of that size. I was well aware of the near impossibility of meeting the deadline, and I couldn't instantly rearrange my work schedule that day to fit it in. In the past, we had not been encouraged to pursue this particular grant, but I got a sense that perhaps the granting committee would be more receptive to us on this round of awards. During the day, I stewed and fretted over the impossibility of getting the application submitted and what this money would mean to PACS if we were awarded the grant. It was a long day, and that night, I finally decided to give it a try. After all, the least they could say was no.

At 10:30 p.m. I got out my laptop, arranged myself comfortably in bed, propped myself among the pillows, prayed, and started writing. I didn't have access to my office files, which would have had the information I needed to easily answer the questions. I simply started writing answers to the questions as they unfolded before me in the application.

I wrote many pages stating why we needed this money. Facts and figures came into my mind as I needed them. I compiled a budget, a projected timeline, equipment needs, and staffing needs. I developed charts and graphs. I tried to think far into the future so that my request would be useful for years to come. I told of board growth, business strategies, and how the agency dreamed of bringing spiritual and physical help to the chronically poor.

My fingers flew. Amazingly, I never had to stop to regroup or grapple with gathering information. Everything seemed to fall into place. I forgot about the time as I wrote from memory and from my heart. Page after page flowed together as the request gelled. After proofreading my work, I was suddenly exhausted.

I yawned for the first time that night and glanced at my clock: it was 3:00 a.m. In just four and a half hours, a complete grant request had materialized, and I had not even gotten sleepy. I settled in for a couple hours of rest. Later that day, I sent it off bearing the coveted postmark that qualified it for review.

I knew from working in the industry that grants written in a hurry were most often of poor quality, things were left out, were poorly conceptualized, and in general were not adequately thought through. Hastily prepared grants were frequently plagued with mathematical mistakes, grammatical errors, and inconsistencies. During the next few weeks, I waited for an answer with fear and trepidation. Finally, the long-anticipated envelope arrived. After taking it to my office, I opened it in private in case my fears were realized. Imagine my joy when I read the first sentence: "We are pleased to grant you $35,000 a year for the next three years for a total of $105,000." I raced out of my office into the receptionist area, waving the letter overhead. Everyone there knew what we had been waiting and praying for, and their joy was even more ecstatic than mine. What a time of praise and celebration we had right then and there amid whoever would join our party.

Over the next three years, that money helped PACS stabilize staffing and funding far beyond what I envisioned that night as I typed God's thoughts. The granting committee probably never realized what a boost they gave to a struggling agency. That grant helped catapult PACS into a time of stability and gave us the opportunity to grow a solid, balanced foundation of the proper ratio of qualified personnel and adequate operational income that is true even today. The Lord wrote that grant through me; I could not have done it on my own. "With God," I have learned, "all things are possible" (Matthew 19:26 NIV).

38

Hug Brings Hope

Lois happily hummed to herself as she busily set about tidying up the greeting cards in our small gift shop. It was a bright morning and a little after opening time, with sunlight streaming through the windows that comprised two walls of the shop. Lois treasured these moments of quietness when she could silently pray and where peace and solitude reigned.

Before long, a customer entered the shop, ending the quiet reverie in which Lois was indulging. Unsuspectingly, as the customer came through the door, she walked through a motion sensor in the shape of a large brown and green toad placed on the floor.

"Ribbit, riiibbbiiitt," croaked the frog loudly.

Startled, the woman laughed good-naturedly. She pointed to the offending creature and exclaimed, "Oh, I didn't see him there. How cute he is!" The woman was very friendly and proceeded to engage Lois in a delightful conversation, acting as if she knew Lois had recognized her. Lois racked her brain to try to remember this woman, but she couldn't figure out where they might have met before this day.

Suddenly and without warning, the lady asked, "Can I give you a hug?"

Lois, by nature a little reserved until she got to know people, was not used to hugging strangers. Her upbringing encouraged a certain amount of polite restraint as acceptable decorum toward strangers, but after pushing those impulses aside, she responded, "Sure!" They shared a long, warm embrace.

"Oh," said the lady, pulling back so she could look Lois squarely in the eye, "I just came in to say, 'Thank you so much.'"

"But why would you thank me? For what? I don't understand," Lois stammered in confusion.

"Let me explain," the lady continued. "My beloved husband of more than fifty years passed away several months ago. One day after he died, I came to this gift shop to look around. It was a particularly rough day for me, and I was grieving. While I was here, you talked with me so gently and with such understanding. I was able to share my feelings, and before I left, you gave me a hug. You have no idea how much that meant to me. Today I just wanted to thank you for your time and that wonderful hug."

"It was my pleasure," Lois responded, even though she honestly did not remember this woman or the day she was describing. "You come back any time. Tell me all about your husband. If he's anything like you, I know he was a wonderful man."

The two women chatted a little longer and ended the visit with another quick hug. The woman left as quickly as she came.

"Ribbit, riiibbbiiitt," the frog croaked dutifully as the woman walked out the door.

Lois returned to her task of straightening up the greeting cards. This time her reflections took a different turn. She shook her head in wonder as she vaguely remembered the Bible text that says good people will live lives that bless others—without even knowing it. Though she didn't look it up, the text can be found in Matthew 25:35–45.

Lois did what came naturally and seemed right. Everyone does this occasionally. Those are the times when we reflect the love of

Jesus. The more we love Him, the more often we will naturally let His love shine through us. It will be like second nature, and we won't even realize we are letting Jesus love others through our actions. Then, like Lois, when someone comes back to thank us, we will be genuinely puzzled and may not remember helping the person. We will be living the biblical scenario, living lives so in tune with Jesus that His wishes will be our natural inclinations.

39

CHAPTER

Work Boots Required

Jeannie was one of those inquisitive volunteers who liked to work in the back room sorting out boxes and bags of donations left by people from all over the Portland metropolitan area. When someone pulled up to the truck-sized, roll-up receiving door, Jeannie would meet them with a grocery cart for their items. Sometimes she would help them unload bulkier items to bring inside the cavernous, industrial-looking receiving area. Everything donated to PACS came through that door.

The original intent of having a twenty-five-foot roll-up receiving door was to bring in the truck at night so we could lock it up to escape vandalism. But when we moved to this new location, our donations increased so much there was never room inside for the truck. The door itself was a major blessing, though, and we never regretted installing it even though it wasn't used the way we had envisioned in our planning.

Beside the door was a doorbell for people to push when they drove up with a donation. Whenever Jeannie heard the doorbell, she would open the door, help the people load their items, and then have them put their name and address on a carbonless duplex paper receipt. She would sign the receipt and give the yellow copy to the donor so they could claim it as a tax-deductible donation. She would put the white copy on a pointed metal spindle with all the other white copies. At the end of the day, the information on the white copies was entered into our software for the accountant's records. We also used those copies to capture new names for our newsletter mailing list. It was a rather tedious process, but it was necessary to keep accurate records of every donation received, cash or non-cash, because our auditors now required that we document donations of all kinds rather than simply tracking cash income and expenses.

One day, Jeannie met a donor at the roll-up receiving door, loaded her cart with the donation, and brought it back to the sorting area. She eagerly started sorting the items. There were a few household items, then clothing, and finally shoes. Among the shoes, she found a pair of brand-new men's boots. News of receiving these boots was worthy of sharing, and she held them high for the other volunteers to see. They got excited and commented to each other.

"Look at how nice they are."

"Wow, we don't hardly ever get men's work boots donated."

"They're huge! What size are they?"

"They must be brand-new."

"And look at this: they have steel toes."

"Wow, someone will be happy to find these; they're expensive in regular stores."

"Let's get them priced and out on the floor with the other men's shoes."

Jeannie finished processing the boots and placed them in a cart with other items. Another volunteer would take them into the main store and put them out for display.

Before long, the interviewing coordinator from a separate part of the building appeared in the thrift store. "Do you have any men's work boots?" she asked the thrift store manager. "I have someone who needs boots. I know we don't usually have any, but I thought I'd check."

"No, we don't have any. Oh, wait a minute—I think some just came out from the sorting area. They were just put on the shelf a few minutes ago," responded the manager. "But they are large, too big for most people."

"Well, let me take them back to the interview room and see if they will fit him. He just got a new job starting tomorrow that requires him to have steel-toed work boots. He's in a predicament because he hasn't earned a paycheck, so he can't go buy new ones. But without boots he can't work to earn a paycheck, so without boots he'll never get paid. It's a vicious circle." She shook her head at the absurdity of it all, even though she understood that jobs came with certain requirements. She briskly walked back to the interview room.

"Here," she told the man. "Try these and see if they'll be okay. It looks like they're brand-new, and they're steel-toed. Let's see if they fit you."

"Well, I'll try," the man said dubiously. "I can almost never find shoes to fit my huge feet." He slipped his feet in effortlessly, and they were the exact size he needed.

It was easy to get used to these kinds of everyday happenings, but even so, each one filled our hearts with amazement at the way God used many people to play a part in His providential care. In the case with these boots, God had already made provision for this man before he'd even asked. If God took care of this man, I know without a doubt He'll most certainly take care of you. He's never too early, and He's never too late.

40

Travel Trailer

I t was late afternoon on a beautiful sunny, warm, summer Friday when the phone rang. I was all by myself at the agency, and I answered it quickly.

"Hi," a man said. "I'm wondering if you accept donations of travel trailers. I have a small one that I don't need anymore."

"Yes," I said, "we accept donations of travel trailers." I didn't tell him that we had never been offered a travel trailer, and I had no idea what we would do with it. We would either give it away or sell it, just like we did with everything else that was donated. Either the donation was a necessity and would be given free to someone, or it could be sold, and the money would be used to help buy food and supplies to support the mission of the agency. I assumed we would set a reasonable price and then wait for the right customer to buy it. No one had ever asked for a travel trailer. He proudly explained to me how he had built it to his own specifications, using his creativity and ingenuity to make it just the way he wanted. He lived over an hour away, so we planned to meet the following Sunday. He would bring the trailer to PACS, and we'd do the necessary paperwork.

When he pulled into the parking lot the next Sunday, I was surprised to see a small, pristine, white, fully homemade travel trailer. It was well built and very clean, and it had everything imaginable to make it comfortable. It was rustic and small but very livable; it was even wired for a surround sound system. He had done a superb job of efficiently building storage and other necessities into little nooks here and there, especially under the king-sized bed. It was fully ready for occupancy.

The next day, Monday, the staff looked at it, excited over this little beauty of a travel trailer. We finally decided it was worth $1,499 which was a fortune to us. We eagerly anticipated the rejoicing that would come the day when someone plunked down the cash for this charming, well-loved treasure.

A few days later, my phone rang again. "Would you be able to help me?" the caller began. "I need help finding housing for Jim, a friend of mine who was recently released from prison. He's on a waiting list for subsidized housing, but it will be months or even years before an apartment will be available to him." I knew the caller was right; the waiting list was over two years to get into federally subsidized housing.

"We can offer him food or medical care," I responded. "But we don't deal with housing. If you'd like, I can put you in touch with other agencies that can help him find housing. Then when he does get an apartment, we can supply furniture and household articles to get him set up comfortably," I commented, satisfied that I'd let the man know how we could help.

The man continued visiting with me, filling me in on the situation. "While Jim is waiting for housing, he is living with my wife and me and our small children. We're happy to help him out, but our house is tiny, and we need a different arrangement. We're very proud of him and the progress he is making since being released from jail. He is attending church with us regularly and becoming very involved in the church life of the congregation. The parishioners have accepted him whole-heartedly. He's quit smoking and is now taking Bible studies."

I congratulated the man on his willingness to help Jim find a new life outside the world that had previously sucked him into making the poor choices leading to his current predicament.

"Oh, it's really exciting to see how well he's doing," the man replied. "We live on a few acres, and we wish somehow that Jim could stay close and keep his connections with the church and his new Christian friends. We're concerned that if he goes to subsidized housing, he may be tempted to return to his old lifestyle."

I then thought of the travel trailer. Perhaps that was why God gave it to us, so we could pass it along to Jim. "We have just received a small travel trailer that might be the answer for you," I offered, silently hoping it wouldn't be what he wanted.

There was a point of angst we sometimes encountered in our agency when an opportunity came to either give something away or to sell it. It was a frequent conversation among the staff and volunteers, and even after praying to know God's thoughts, not everyone was always unified on the same conclusion every time. It often seemed to me that it would be better to turn these items into cash rather than let them be used by one person. But knowing the Lord might have plans other than mine concerning the trailer, I continued. "It would be a perfect place for Jim to have his own space. It was built to be a man-cave and has heat, and the roof is sturdy; it won't leak if Jim needs to use it in the winter. I think it would work very well for him while he waits for permanent housing."

"Oh, that's perfect!" the man exclaimed. "That's exactly what we need! Thank you, Jesus, for providing the solution for Jim and for my family. You did it before we even asked." Then he turned back to me and asked hesitatingly, "How much are you selling it for?"

I answered unreservedly and almost gleefully, "The trailer is all yours, free. Just come and get it!" That was exactly what happened. A couple days later, the man came, hooked up the trailer, and took it home to Jim. Though I've never heard the end of the story, I can only assume the Lord is still working out the events of Jim's life and in the lives of those who love him.

As I reminisce about this experience, I thank the Lord for reminding me that God loves those who give cheerfully (2 Corinthians 9:7). The Lord is amazing in the way He gently weaves together circumstances to teach us lessons while fulfilling His divine plans for His beloved children.

41

CHAPTER

Now She's Gone

Fred was what the workers called a regular at the thrift store. A regular was someone who came often, sometimes every day or even several times a day. The workers enjoyed the regulars because of the close relationships that often developed through the increased opportunities to become acquainted. Fred enjoyed wandering up and down the aisles, sometimes finding a treasure to buy but often not. The thrift store was usually bustling with activity, which gave him time to browse. Other times, when things were not so busy, he would visit with the volunteers and others who worked there. Most of the time, he was somewhat reserved.

This day, as he slowly closed the door behind him, Fred could see things were busy in the thrift store. The clerks greeted him and let him look around. Taking his time, he aimlessly wandered up and down the aisles. He seemed preoccupied, almost absent.

Then he entered the gift shop. The gift shop was new to him. It was pleasantly decorated, smelled like vanilla candles, and had soft Christian music playing in the background. He had never come in this part before; he'd always thought this stuff was more for his wife. He could tell everything in the gift shop was brand-new.

The greeting cards, the bird baths, the brightly colored slippers, the beautiful vases and dishes—all created a serene and restful atmosphere. No one else was shopping here right now. He stood lost in thought, looking around vacantly.

"Good morning, how are you?" the clerk said cheerfully. When he didn't respond, she took a closer look. Noticing his dejection, she asked, "Are you all right?"

"No, I'm not good at all," Fred replied. "My wife died yesterday. We were married sixty-three years. She was my best friend. I took her to the hospital, but I never thought she wouldn't come home. She was only there a day. Now she's gone." He continued to talk about their life together. He talked of the children they'd always wanted but never had. He talked of how they'd loved holding hands and walking on the beach, how they'd enjoyed traveling, and what a good schoolteacher she had been. He struggled to talk in past tense because the loss was so fresh and the wound so raw.

The clerk visited with him for a long time and then asked if she could give him a hug. He accepted the warm gesture in his characteristically reserved manner. Then he turned to go. "Thanks," he said simply.

That was the start of Fred becoming more of a regular than ever. Every day he came just to talk. He talked to the workers, the clerks, the chaplain, and the other volunteers. He was always a gentleman, grateful for the connection with friends who would take time to listen over and over. He hated the weekends when the store was closed. Over the months, occasionally Fred began to miss a day, then a couple days. He gradually resumed the schedule he had kept before his wife died. His step lightened, and his eyes brightened ever so gradually. We loved seeing the new him.

Fred blessed us with his friendship even during this difficult time. We hope we were a blessing to him as well. Fred didn't need a clothes closet, where he could receive free clothing once a month; he had enough money to buy his own. Fred needed someone to listen. He needed friendship. That's the beauty of thrift and gift ministries: customers come as often as they like. There's always a chance they will become a regular, and a new friendship will be born.

42

CHAPTER

Natalie on the Bus

Natalie gazed out at the bright sunshine. The kids were still asleep. No sense waking them up. The cupboards were empty, so there wouldn't be any breakfast. Let them sleep, if possible.

It seemed like a nightmare. Her husband had left a year ago. Her housekeeping job at the hotel was steady but was only minimum wage. It was hard feeding and clothing the kids and paying rent. Last week, she'd spent almost all her check on rent. The next day, her boss called her in. She couldn't remember it all—something about not enough business lately; cutting back. But one thing was clear: her job was gone.

A whimper came from the bedroom. The baby must be waking. Natalie worried about Sarah. Just thirteen months old, Sarah was coughing a lot lately and pulling at her ears. Nathan, nine years old, seemed serious beyond his years, especially now. Nathan and his older sister, Heather, eleven years old, would need school clothes in two weeks.

Natalie scooped Sarah from her crib and cuddled her soothingly as only a caring mother could. Her mind went back to Nathan and

Heather. School clothes—she'd forgotten about that. What was she going to do? Suddenly the gravity of her situation struck.

"Oh, God," she breathed as she sank into a chair. "Oh, God, take care of us."

She hadn't heard Heather and Nathan until they trooped sleepily into the living room where she was cuddling Sarah. "Mom, we're hungry."

"I know, honey," replied Natalie. "We don't have any food here, but we're going to do something special," she said, suddenly brightening. "We're going to get on the bus and go find food. Jesus will give us food."

Surprised at her own words, she went into action. She quickly she dressed Sarah while Heather and Nathan excitedly dressed themselves. The family walked down to the bus stop, and after a short wait, they boarded the bus. Without a destination in mind, they simply rode. They traveled for what seemed a long time. The driver noticed they didn't seem to have a place to get off and seemed to be just riding. He visited amiably with Natalie and gently asked her a few questions. When the bus was nearly empty, Natalie found herself opening her heart.

"When I went to work yesterday, they laid me off because they don't need a full crew right now." She tried to talk softly so Nathan and Heather couldn't hear her. "I had just paid my rent, and I was going to buy groceries with my next check. Now I have no money to buy groceries, pay next month's rent, get the kids school clothes, or take my baby to the doctor. My kids are hungry, but there isn't any food in the house, so I told them we're going on an adventure. That's why we are all on the bus, but I don't know where we should get off."

The bus driver didn't say a lot and nodded a few times in sympathetic agreement. A couple blocks later, he pulled over to the curb and stopped the bus. "Okay," he said cheerily to the children, "it's time for you to get off." He quietly told Natalie, "Get off here, and they'll help you. They help anyone no matter where they come from or what their religion."

Natalie obediently got off, somewhat in a daze. What was this place? The sun was hot, and little Sarah kept crying. Suddenly Natalie felt tired. She gathered her courage. Her children were hungry and sick, and above all, she determined they would somehow stay in their apartment. She looked up and read uncomprehendingly, "Portland Adventist Community Services."

She shyly pushed open the door and entered what seemed to be a waiting room. The receptionist warmly greeted her and the children. Soon they were ushered into a small room where an interviewer listened carefully, gently encouraging Natalie to tell her story. For the second time that morning, it all tumbled out. "We're so hungry. We got on the bus with nowhere to go, and we ended up here."

Jumping into action, the interviewer immediately gathered sandwiches and fruit so they could eat. When they finished, Natalie was taken to the grocery warehouse where she could choose things for her family, even formula and diapers for Sarah. Natalie could tell PACS lived the values they displayed on the wall: dignity, education, and compassion.

The interviewer noticed the baby was feverish, so he took Natalie into the health clinic, where the volunteer doctor diagnosed an ear infection and gave Natalie samples from the clinic pharmacy to treat it. But Natalie's visit was not finished. From the health clinic, Natalie was taken into the thrift shop so Nathan and Heather could choose two complete outfits to get them ready for school. Natalie also chose clothes for job hunting, or maybe to go to school herself, as suggested by the interviewer.

Overwhelmed, Natalie kept saying, "I can't believe it. God sent me here. God sent me here. I have received everything I need." Her tears spoke more eloquently than her words.

What happened to Natalie? She came back about a year later. Her new outfit gave away her news. "I was able to get welfare support so I could go to school. I graduated with a certificate, and now I have a job," she said, beaming. She managed to keep her apartment and was supporting her family. She didn't need help anymore.

"You helped me, and now I want to help someone else," she explained as she handed over a bag of clothes and toys.

43

CHAPTER ━━━━━━━━━━━━━━━━━━━━━

Depression Gone

A ccess to medical care has become increasingly difficult for many people. Historically, medical care was provided by family physicians who often came to people's home, making house calls. The family paid the doctor in whatever arrangement they worked out together. Over the years, it became the norm to treat people in offices, clinics, and hospitals, where medical equipment and a wide array of medications were more readily available. Billing was still directly to the patient, but costs were increasing and beginning to burden families. Health insurance companies sprang up, offering to shoulder the growing burden of health care in return for monthly payments from families and individuals. In time, employers embraced the practice of paying employees' health care insurance premiums to offer employees a benefit rather than increasing their wages. These premiums were often more cost effective when bundled as a group through an employer than as a single individual or family.

Medical care grew increasingly complicated, with huge costs involving the hospitals and doctors. Lawsuits became popular, and medical liability insurance for professionals added to the cost of health care. The government became involved, developing plans like Medicare and Medicaid. After a while, Oregon developed its own state-sponsored Oregon Health Plan (OHP). The OHP was designed to cover health care and pharmaceutical costs for the poorest of the poor. If people had any income at all, they were not eligible for the OHP, and certainly not if health care was provided by their employers. The OHP was the pride of many of the state lawmakers and created a certain measure of stability for those who had not been able to afford medical insurance or health care in the past. The plan worked well when it was funded adequately, but state politics changed, and funding fluctuated. It was at those times that the OHP created extremely difficult circumstances for the very people it was intended to help.

When Kris, a fifty-one-year-old single woman, lost access to her medications due to cuts in the OHP, the results were devastating. Kris was diagnosed with bipolar disorder. Without medication, she would swing from manic episodes of feeling high or euphoric, where she would talk abnormally fast and hardly ever sleep, to lows of severe depression. The highs could last several months, and so could the lows.

The lows were the worst. She would go several months suffering deep depression, and she experienced debilitating hallucinations. Sometimes she would stay in bed for days at a time. She didn't cook or clean, and she'd tried to commit suicide during her last bout with depression. Kris tried getting help at several free or low-cost clinics, but no one could assist her without payment for her medications. She felt she had nowhere to go.

Fortunately, Kris heard about PACS Family Health Clinic and thought she would try one more time to get help. During that time, one of the nurses at the clinic was working very hard to help patients access pharmaceutical drug programs offered for impoverished individuals. It was not easy because there was a lot of repetitive monthly paperwork, as well as technological obstacles for patients. Many of them were not able to navigate the process without help, and this nurse set about to make sure that anyone who qualified and wanted the help was able to receive medication.

Kris was very motivated, and with the aid of the nurse at the clinic and the pharmaceutical drug program, she was able to get back on her medications. Even when she finally got back on her medicines, it was a long, uphill struggle. We had no psychiatric support for patients, and Kris had no insurance for mental health care or psychotropic medications. The entire staff at the clinic poured themselves into helping Kris with her journey back to manageable health. Though it wasn't recommended or standard practice, some of the staff gave Kris their home phone numbers so she could reach them whenever she felt she was in crisis. Many times, sometimes even in the middle of the night, Kris would call the volunteer doctor at home, and he would calm her fears. Ever so gradually, she began to improve.

After many months, the hallucinations quit coming. Kris began to sleep normally. Her speech was not so rapid, she spoke at appropriate times, and she began behaving in more socially accepted patterns. She started taking care of herself physically and mentally, and the fog of her depression lifted. It was a long process, but it was very rewarding to the clinic team to see the transformation in Kris. The nurse managing the pharmaceutical medication program continued to support Kris, helping her stay current on her paperwork to get her medications. It became obvious Kris did not need to see the doctor regularly other than to support her medication management.

Kris was so grateful that she brought a note with her on her last visit, thanking them for treating her with professionalism, giving her dignity, and giving her a new outlook on life.

44

CHAPTER ════════════════════

Christmas Past
Made Better

Ten-year-old Lou was over-the-top excited. She loved school, and today her teacher announced that on Friday of next week, Lou's fourth-grade class would have a Christmas party. In preparation for the party, the teacher had the children draw the name of another student for whom they were to bring a gift. Lou could hardly wait for the school day to finish so she could tell her mother. Finally, the afternoon was over, and the students were dismissed. Lou rushed home to tell her mother the wonderful news.

Mother realized this was a momentous occasion for Lou. But Mother knew what Lou did not know: there was no money to buy gifts for her family this year, much less an additional gift for a school party. Lou's mother wanted Lou to be able to participate in the gift exchange, and she was a resourceful and creative woman. She went to work to make sure Lou had a gift to take to school the next Friday.

Lou's mother searched the house until she found a lovely picture, one which she felt would be just right for a fourth grader. She glued it carefully to some cardboard, taking extreme care so that it would be perfectly flat with no bubbles or creases. Then she got out her sharpest scissors and painstakingly cut the cardboard with the picture on it into jigsaw pieces that fit together to make a perfect puzzle. Lou's eyes danced as she and her mother carefully wrapped the gift for the party. Lou could imagine the look of wonder on the face and the squeal of delight of the little girl whose name Lou had drawn as the other child opened this most treasured gift. She lovingly carried the gift to the party.

Finally, the moment came for the gift to be opened. Lou found herself clutching her hands together and dancing up and down with anticipation as the other student opened the gift. The other girl took so long to open her present. Lou excitedly held her breath. Finally, the girl opened the box to reveal the puzzle so carefully and wondrously made. Lou's eyes opened wide with unbelief as she saw the little girl's lips curl in disgust at what she called "such a shabby thing." The look on her face changed everything Lou had eagerly anticipated. That look stabbed Lou like a dagger, piercing straight to her heart. The little girl promptly dumped it in the trash. Lou's excitement turned to bitter disappointment; stinging tears filled her eyes and escaped down her cheeks. This had to be the worst day of her life.

Mother was hurt and disappointed, both for herself but mostly for her daughter. She tried to console Lou as only a mother could, but she could not remove the bruises from Lou's heart. Even now, occasionally around Christmas, as a grown adult, Lou vividly relived this experience. The memories of that shocking experience dug up the old wounds, and the hurt was fresh again.

One Christmas, after Lou grew up and she had the money to buy Christmas presents, that experience came back to haunt her. She vowed on that Christmas she would give a gift to a little girl that would make Christmas the happiest day of that little girl's life. But what could she give? To whom would she give it? She didn't know any fourth-grade girls that needed anything, so Lou brought her money to PACS, requesting that we find a little fourth grade girl and get her what she needed for Christmas.

We were excited about this once-in-a-lifetime opportunity for a little girl, and we knew just whom to contact. We reached out to an inner-city fourth-grade teacher to get her recommendation about this special situation. The teacher suggested we consider Heather as a suitable candidate. Heather loved artwork, drawing, and creating. She was especially skilled and dreamed of having her own computer and becoming a graphic artist. Without special intervention and outside help, Heather would never be able to gain the skills she needed to build a foundation to move her toward her dreams.

Lou agreed with this suggestion, but her gift alone could not cover the expense. Others learned about this project and offered to help. Someone went to a local computer company, which agreed to cover the rest of the cost, and soon Heather received her own computer. Lou did not wish Heather to know about her gift, so the teacher had to relay Heather's response back to us.

The teacher reported that Heather was ecstatic with the gift. She regularly uses the computer and software. Heather's older siblings use the computer in their schoolwork as well, and Heather is becoming computer literate—a most important skill these days. Thank you, Lou, for caring, sharing, and reaching out. The hurt in your heart turned into a desire to create happiness, and hopefully it brought healing to you.

45

CHAPTER

What Do You Need?

A man walked into the thrift store looking dirty, grimy, tattered, and worn. His disheveled appearance belied the sophistication with which he spoke. His unshaven face, careworn and smudged, told of difficult times, but he made no complaint. He was downcast and apologetic.

"Please," he said. "I have a chance for a job interview. I used to work, and I need to look sharp. Can you help me?"

Elaine, the manager of our thrift ministry, quickly assessed him for the proper size. After all, it was more than a store—it was a ministry. The real reason for distributing clothes and household items through a thrift store venue was to be a place where anyone would feel comfortable. People could come without having to accept charity. Others who needed a bit of a boost could also come.

"Sure," she answered. "What kind of things do you need?" This was an important question aimed at allowing individuals to articulate their needs and wants, rather than us assuming we knew what they needed.

Elaine helped the man find things that fit him and that he felt represented him well in his upcoming job interview. He chose a full set of clothes complete with shoes and socks.

"Do you have anything I could use to get cleaned up?" he asked, again somewhat apologetic.

"Absolutely, I have just what you need," Elaine responded. She gave him soap, toothbrush, and a razor and wished him well.

Instead of leaving, the man disappeared into the bathroom. He was there a long time. After a while, he emerged. He had completely washed, shaved, and donned his new clothes. He beamed at himself in the mirror on the bathroom door before he sat down in the chair Elaine provided, and then he put on his new socks and shoes.

Elaine later recounted, "Everything about his appearance totally changed. He looked me in the eye with pride. No longer was he ashamed and apologetic. He held his head high."

He profusely thanked Elaine and took off proudly down the street. Elaine never heard whether he got the job.

When Elaine told me this story, it reminded me of another incident I had handled quite differently. The occasion taught me an important lesson I've never forgotten.

It was a cold winter morning. Snow blanketed the ground, somewhat muting the sounds of cars honking and splashing through puddles in the streets. The line of people bundled up in coats and scarves needing food had slowly diminished. Nearly everyone had been interviewed, and the last few were sitting along the wall for a short wait before entering the food pantry.

I walked through the food pantry waiting area on my way to the health clinic. One of the people waiting was Jack, someone I recognized because he came every month. He was disabled and on permanent government subsidy. It wasn't much, so he was forced to supplement his food supply and help make his food dollars stretch to cover the weeks. He was dressed in cotton shorts and a short-sleeved cotton shirt. Noting his obvious lack of appropriate clothes for the cold weather, I made a mental note to come back and talk with him when I'd finished my business in the health clinic.

On my return trip, I engaged Jack in conversation. We talked about the weather and how cold it was. It was a perfect segue for me to broach the subject I wanted to discuss. "Jack," I began awkwardly, "I know it's cold outside."

He looked at me quizzically. "What about it?"

"Well, I see you're wearing shorts, and I wondered if you would like a pair of warmer pants and a warmer shirt." I plunged into my topic. "We could find you something in the thrift store, if you'd like." I could sense his discomfort, but I was pleased with myself that I'd noticed and offered him what he plainly needed.

He was not happy with my offer. "So you think you know what I need, huh?" He spat the words at me. "Why do people always think they know what's best for me? Why can't people ask me what I think I need? How do you know I even want different pants? I don't need warmer pants. I'm very comfortable the way I am. Thank you very much for your warm-hearted charity," he finished sarcastically.

Stunned, I realized I deserved his rebuke. I had not given him the dignity of living life his way. If he wanted to wear short pants in the snow, that was up to him. I had assumed he didn't have any other pants to wear, which was demeaning to him. He hadn't asked for clothes, only food, and I should have respected his desires without pushing my ideas on him.

I applaud Elaine for having the sensitivity to ask what the man needed when he came for clothes for his job interview. It is easy to assume we know what people need, but we don't walk in their shoes. We don't live their lives. We can't accurately judge when they make decisions that seem foolish to a middle-class mind-set. If we are ever in their circumstances, we may choose to do life just as they do because maybe, just maybe, it works best that way.

The moral of the story? As Jesus did when He was on earth, I've learned to always ask what people would like to have rather than telling them what they need. I'd recommend that you do so too. You may be very surprised at their answers.

CHAPTER 46

Luann and Shelter

Luann was deliriously happy. She had finally married Jorge, the man of her dreams. Not only was Jorge stunningly good looking, but he was a perfect gentleman. Luann was not a bad find herself, as Jorge's friends raucously pointed out to him. Petite and witty with long blonde hair, Luann could hold her own wherever she went. As a couple, they were the life of every party.

And parties there were—lots of them. At first it was exciting, even exhilarating, to party all night. Booze and drugs flowed freely until the parties wound down in the early hours of the morning, and then everyone would somehow find their way home. This was the way Jorge and Luann spent the first few months of their marriage. It seemed like a dream come true to Luann, even though Jorge didn't seem to handle the booze and drugs very well.

When Luann and Jorge would return home in the wee hours of the morning, Jorge would often become angry. He accused Luann of flirting with the other guys at the party and threatened to beat her up if it happened again. She repeated over and over that she had eyes only for him, tearfully promising to never again look like she might be interested in someone else. After every party, the same argument would erupt, and soon Jorge was making good on his threats, punctuating his accusations with punches and kicks. They argued more and more until the neighbors called the authorities to report the screaming, yelling, and crying they heard coming from Jorge and Luann's apartment.

Luann's dream of a happy marriage quickly unraveled. She found herself hiding her bruises and defending Jorge to her friends. She dreaded the evenings and weekends when the violence seemed to never end. Even Jorge admitted to being unhappy with the way they were living. In a rare moment of lucidity, they agreed to move away from the town. They would leave the parties, the friends, and all the bad memories and start over. After all, they loved each other.

Luann and her husband decided to drive to Portland, hoping things would get better. Instead, when they were driving through town at nearly midnight, a violent argument erupted between them. As they traveled down a freeway, Jorge slammed on the brakes, pulled over, and stopped the car. In a fit of anger, he ran around the car and threw opened Luann's door. With a string of vulgar profanities, he yanked her out of the car, throwing her roughly to the ground. "And take this," he snarled, giving one more kick to Luann's quivering body crumpled in the gravel.

With that, Jorge jumped back into the car, stomped on the gas pedal, and angrily sped away, the tires squealing on the wet pavement. Stunned, sobbing, and hurting, Luann lay by the side of the freeway until she could recover from the shock of this unexpected turn of events. There were almost no other cars on the road, and those that flew by didn't seem to notice her thin and trembling body in the gravel just off the side of the pavement.

Portland was a new town to her. She didn't know where to go or what to do. It was cold and drizzly, not at all like the balmy nights she was used to in Southern California. She got up shivering, pulling her T-shirt around her as best she could. Then she began to walk. The walking helped keep her warm, but it was also scary. She was in a strange town all by herself in the darkest hours of the night. She was not accustomed to the dangers that lurked in Portland. She fearfully headed for the nearest exit and then wandered here and there, taking streets that led her away from the freeway so Jorge couldn't come back and find her.

Not knowing what to do or where to go, Luann spent the whole night wandering the streets. In the morning, cold and hungry, frightened and bruised, she found herself aimlessly walking in front of PACS. She saw it was a place where people seemed to be congregating, so she thought maybe she might at least slip in and get warm for a while.

She was surprised at the friendliness of the people and soon blurted her story to the thrift shop cashier. When the cashier learned of Luann's plight, he called for help from the social service manager. Before long, Luann had been given a coat and warm, dry clothes. The social service manager found her some breakfast and visited with her until she warmed up and began to feel better.

Luann pleaded for help. She was afraid Jorge might find her. His abusiveness had escalated over the months, and after being thrown out on the freeway, she feared for her life. She was afraid to leave, and the social service manager was afraid to let her leave. After many phone calls, using the connections forged with other agencies over the years, the social service manager found another agency that could keep Luann safe while she found some direction for her life. With food in her stomach, Luann left PACS in the care of someone sent from the other agency, moved into a shelter, and began receiving help dealing with her abuse.

This story lingers with me. I could tell you other stories very much like this. I can only imagine how many times this tragic scenario plays out across our nation every day, every night. Violence and abuse are rampant, fed by vice and addictions. When does it stop? Who is there to help? When will my heart no longer ache over these memories? I can only do my part and leave the justice to the Lord. After all, He promises in His word, "Vengeance is mine; I will repay" (Romans 12:19 KJV).

47

CHAPTER

Cold Kids, Warm Hearts

❝ Hello? Hi? Knock-knock? Is anybody here?" The knocking at the back door was insistent, obviously coming from whoever belonged to the face peering intently through the narrow perpendicular window of the gray metal door.

"I'm sorry, but we're closed," explained Peter through the locked door. He was putting away food that had been picked up from local stores that morning. He opened the door a crack to explain, "The volunteers couldn't get here because of the blowing snow and strong winds. I am only here for a couple of minutes. Can you come back when we are open?"

"Okay," replied the boy, trying to act older than his teenage years. He turned into the biting wind, wrapping his arm protectively around the thin, young girl with him. They moved together out into the empty, snowy parking lot without complaint or comment. Peter lingered at the open door, watching them lean into the bone-chilling cold and recede slowly into the grayness of the morning. It was eerily quiet outside, snow was falling, the wind was still for a few minutes, and he realized there was almost no traffic in the normally busy street nearby; even the buses were on snow routes.

He felt bad for turning away the kids. He noticed they had no hats or gloves, and their coats were thin; it crossed his mind that they might be in danger of hypothermia. *They're probably hungry too*, he thought.

He finished his work quickly, carefully made his way through the ice and snow to his car, and prepared to drive away. The driveway passed by the front of the building where he had been working. The big plate glass windows revealed clothes, couches, pictures, and other secondhand items on sale in the thrift store. It was dark inside, closed because driving conditions were too dangerous for volunteers to make it in to run the cash registers. The beige, cement-block building had been renovated from a grocery store. It boasted a flat roof and two alcoves on each side of the picture windows with doors for entry and exit. There, in the alcove nearest the bus stop, he saw the two teenagers huddled on the cement by the door, hoping to gain a bit of protection from the wind chill factor of four degrees Fahrenheit. They had nowhere to go, and at least this gave them a little shelter. Gusts of wind occasionally picked up leaves and other debris, swirling it about them; they shielded their faces as they turned toward the building.

Suddenly suffering from acute remorse, he pulled his car over and asked, "Are you hungry?"

"Oh, yes, mister," they replied. "We haven't eaten for a long time. We have no place to stay. We were under a bridge last night, but it was so cold we couldn't sleep. Just a little bit to eat would be very nice." They were polite, not asking for much and grateful for anything.

"Jump in," said Peter. "Let me get you something." He put the kids in his car, did a U-turn, and swung around behind the building to the door he had just locked.

As he struggled to unlock the door for them, another car pulled around into the parking lot. A woman Peter had never seen before pulled up beside the door and asked, "What's going on here?" Peter was surprised because the back door of the building could not be seen from the street. *How did this woman know there was anyone here? What does she mean by "What's going on here?"* he thought fleetingly, but he didn't ask her any questions. Her car was not fancy, but it seemed clean and reliable.

"These kids are hungry, and I'm getting ready to feed them," answered Peter. The lady persisted, asking more and more questions until she understood the teens were both hungry and homeless. She reached in vain for her cell phone.

"Can I come in and use your phone?" she asked. "I want to call my landlord and see if he will let me take them home with me for a couple of nights." Sure enough, the landlord agreed to the plan. "Everything is good!" announced the lady brightly, suddenly commanding authority. "Now, give me some spaghetti to feed these kids. All kids like pasta!" The two young teenagers were given sandwiches to eat immediately, and then they were whisked away to a warm apartment where their hostess was able to feed them a warm dinner from the generous supply Peter provided.

Peter was astounded at the turn of events. He had helped lots of people get food; in fact, he'd helped so many that sometimes he wondered whether they were really hungry or simply using the system. He had never seen those kids before. He had never seen the lady before; in fact, he'd forgotten to even ask her for her name. What if Peter had ignored the Holy Spirit whispering in the back of his mind to let in the kids and give them food? What if he had ignored his guilt, shoved it to the back of his mind, and driven away, disappearing down the empty, icy street?

The fact is that any of us could find ourselves in Peter's shoes. Could it possibly be that we might get so callous in our work of helping people that it seems few are really needy? When Peter reminisced about this experience, he wondered whether that lady was an angel. She drove past the front doors to the back parking lot even though she could see the place was closed. Her timing was more than a coincidence, fortuitous, meant to be, serendipitous, or however best these times are described. To Peter, it was providential and miraculous. And he wondered, *How many landlords would willingly allow a tenant to bring teenage strangers off the street to their apartment for one night, much less several?* He shook his head in awe.

We are grateful the Lord intervenes at times to keep His children safe. Thank You, God, for speaking to Peter. Thank you, Peter, for listening.

48

CHAPTER

TV Is a Necessity

It was a nasty divorce. The court battle was long and expensive. George's ex-wife made hard bargains, and he felt he had come out the loser financially and emotionally. But the worst thing was that his ex-wife received full custody of their two boys with only sporadic visiting rights for him.

George was devastated by this turn of events because he loved his boys more than anything else in the world. For George, not being with his boys was like turning off the sun forever. He couldn't handle this blow and decided to leave Oregon and move to California. The move was good for George, and he started making plans to get a job and settle down.

But no sooner had he arrived in California than he learned his wife was unexpectedly giving up custody of their sons. Immediately, George repacked his suitcase and returned to Oregon. He had new energy; his boys, only six and eight years old, needed him. His first job, however, was to convince the judge that he was capable of being the dad his boys needed. His ex-wife's family was planning on making a case that the boys should be given into the custody of their mother's sister, a plan that George could not bear to even imagine. *Take my boys away? Never again!* he resolved.

Fearing for his children's future, George immediately landed a job and rented an apartment. He had to show the court he was employed and had adequate housing for his boys. The judge was pleased with his resourcefulness, his obvious love, and his ability to care for the boys and granted him custody of his sons. George thought he would be overjoyed and overcome with relief.

However, instead of happy anticipation, George felt numb. The boys were arriving in four short days. The judge knew he had an apartment, but what the judge did not know was that the apartment was bare. George had no furniture at all. He barely had clothes, only the ones he had stuffed into his suitcase.

George was frightened. What would the boys sleep in? What would the boys sit on? What would they eat out of? He couldn't begin to think of all the things he would need to create a home for two small boys. His sparse wallet was no help.

George's story was an exciting challenge to the PACS team. An empty apartment meant an opportunity to fill rooms and touch people's lives. What fun we had, scurrying around and exploring with George the things he might need. He chose three beds, a kitchen table and chairs, living room furniture, dishes, pots and pans, a toaster, towels and blankets, and whatever else he would need to fill his apartment with the basics of everyday living.

But George was still not satisfied. Puzzled and looking at the immense pile of necessities set aside to load in his truck, I inquired what else he needed.

"I see you have a TV," George said. "Could we add the TV to these things?"

What? I thought. *This man has a huge pile of furniture, kitchen items, and linens, and he wants a television?* The rule of thumb we followed when helping people get settled in new housing was that we were happy to give them what they needed, but we drew the line at things that were not "necessities." My mind struggled to understand how a television was a need rather than a want. I feared George was taking advantage of our generosity.

I explained our philosophy to George, telling him we would not be able to let him have the TV and ending with a question. "Do you really believe a TV is necessary for human survival?"

George politely and patiently enlightened me on his need of a TV. He explained, "I work all day. I can't be home in the afternoons when the boys get home from school. I can't afford childcare; I can't afford a babysitter, and I can't leave them in an empty apartment by themselves with nothing to do. They are six and eight years old, and they need entertainment until I can get there. I will be home within an hour of when they come home. I need the television to be my babysitter."

I realized he was telling the truth. He was right. For him, a television was a need. Even though I didn't like the thought of the boys being by themselves, that arrangement was going to be reality for George and his family until he could get his hours changed. The boys needed to be occupied until their dad could get home. George had already thought it all out and come up with a solution to his babysitting problem.

For the first time ever, I sent a TV home with someone, and I considered it as necessary as food or clothing. This experience presented me with a moral conundrum and taught me the importance of flexibility in applying our man-made rules to situations. More important than any rule is to meet people where they are in the spectrum of options they have available.

49

CHAPTER

Ominous Knock

M any adventures began at PACS with the ringing of the phone, and this case was no exception. "I would like to donate a car to you," stated the voice on the other end of the line. This was always good news and has been a wonderful source of income for PACS over the years.

Per usual, we accepted the car, searched the Internet to find an approximate value, and then posted the determined price in the driver's side window and in the front windshield. We were very blessed to be located on a busy street where people could easily see the cars we had for sale. The car was parked in its designated space by the street where everyone driving by could see the sale sign.

A couple days later, when he had more time, the volunteer responsible for determining car prices took it for a test drive to see how it ran. *Uh-oh*, he thought. *I think I hear something that isn't right.* He drove it around the block again to confirm his suspicions. Yes, there was an ominous knock in the engine. How disappointing. We didn't fix cars, and this car would not be useable for very long without some major repairs. The body was in excellent condition, so he had originally priced it on the high side, assuming it would be as good on the inside as it looked on the outside. Reluctantly, he substantially dropped the price.

When he relayed this disappointing turn of events to Lori, the thrift store manager, she made new signs to replace the ones in the windows of the car. Lori and the other volunteer were a little deflated over this turn of events because they had anticipated making good money on the car.

Lori grabbed the new signs to take out to the car, but she got busy for a few minutes inside the store, so the new signs were forgotten for the moment. She waited on a couple customers, frustrated that she could not get the new price posted on the car. Before long, Lori had almost finished waiting on people; only one more couple, a woman in a wheelchair with her husband, wanted to ask her a question.

"We see you have a car for sale," they began. "We need a car. It looks nice and would fit our needs perfectly. Could you tell us a little bit about it?"

Lori told the lady and her husband what she knew about the car and about the knock in the engine.

"Do you mind if I take it for a test drive?" the husband requested. "I'd like to hear what it's doing."

"Of course you may," Lori responded, and she rushed to get the keys.

After a brief test spin around the large parking lot, he returned undaunted. "I've worked on cars a lot," he declared. "I'm sure I can fix the problem, and it will purr like a kitten."

The couple assumed the price was what was originally posted in the car window, so their first question was, "Will you take a partial payment up front, and then we will pay you the rest later?" This was not an option for Lori because it was strictly against our thrift store policies to sell anything on a payment basis. She explained the policy, adding, "Before you came in, we had dropped the price on the car because of the knocking in the engine. I haven't had a chance to post the new price on the car, so the car is cheaper than the price you see posted on it now. Would that be helpful?"

"Oh, praise the Lord," they exclaimed. 'We need a car so badly. We haven't had one for several months and have been praying to God every day for a way to get around." They were praying the Lord would lead them to just the right car, one they could afford and still have money for medicine and food. They had saved carefully over the last nine months, which was enough to cover the down payment they had originally offered to Lori.

Lori took the couple back to her desk so they could talk more. The woman opened her purse and pulled out their car savings. The couple counted it carefully in disbelief. They had just enough money to cover the reduced price of the car, plus insurance.

With great joy they paid in full, called to set up insurance, and drove the car off the lot. They weren't the only ones thanking God for their car. Lori and the volunteer in charge of setting car prices rejoiced as they realized that God had intended this car for a specific couple who had finally saved enough money.

50

CHAPTER

Head Start Physicals

The three little girls giggled and whispered, waiting nervously for the doctor. They were sisters aged three, four, and five and had come for Head Start physicals. Their black hair glistened, matching their big, dark, sparkling eyes.

Head Start physicals were required for acceptance into the local Head Start program, a branch of the United States Department of Health and Human Services. This program was intended to support low-income children ages newborn to five, and their families, to help them be ready for school. Each year the local program partnered with the health clinic to provide free physicals to children of low-income families. A clean bill of health from the health clinic meant the children could attend preschool and other activities made available to help the children maintain a developmental path that would help them with readiness for school.

On this day, the girls, Rosa, Anna, and Lucia, wiggled and squirmed, their little bodies squeezed into two light mauve, cushioned, plastic chairs that were connected with a silver, aluminum-braced arm at each end, topped with a wooden arm rest. They entertained themselves as best they could, but it seemed like they had to wait a long time. Their mother was patient with them, glancing at the clock and silently wishing the time would pass more quickly.

Finally, the mother and her little girls were ushered into an exam room. Soon the doctor came in. He was struck by the bright eyes and quick smiles of the girls, who didn't seem to be shy; they entered into easy conversation with him. He did what all doctors have done for decades and centuries when examining their patients.

First, he examined Rosa, the oldest. He poked and thumped, and he looked down her throat and in her ears. Then he got out his funny-looking stethoscope, put it in his ears, and began to listen to her lungs. "Take a deep breath," he said. "Now let it out." In, out; in, out. After he had examined her lungs, the doctor asked Rosa to be very quiet so he could listen to her heart. Then it was Anna's turn.

The doctor followed the same process with Anna, poking, probing, looking, asking Anna to breathe in and out, and then listening to her heart. Anna was nervous and glad when the doctor was finished.

Then he asked three-year-old Lucia to hop up on the exam table. Once again, he followed the same sequence, poking, probing, looking, asking Lucia to breathe in and out, and listening to her heart. But wait—Lucia's heart didn't sound quite right. He listened some more. No, it was not right.

When the doctor finished examining the girls, he spoke to the mother privately. He explained he was hearing an abnormality in Lucia's heart and carefully outlined the details of how he wanted to get additional testing done to confirm his suspicions. The mother agreed, and so began a long journey for a very little girl.

The doctor referred Lucia to Oregon Health Sciences University (OHSU), where they were equipped to treat cases like Lucia's. The health clinic enjoyed a congenial relationship with OHSU and often referred cases to them that needed more intense follow-up than our clinic could provide. The university always provided this care at no charge to our clinic patients.

OHSU could take Lucia the next day. Just as the clinic doctor suspected, the university doctors found a definite malfunction in her heart. She was scheduled for surgery, which went well. After many months of treatment, she was finally released under close supervision. She would need to be monitored carefully each year to make sure her heart developed properly to support her physical growth.

Of course, this was something her parents never expected. As all parents would in this situation, they welcomed and received special training to learn how to help Lucia live a normal life as a child, and through the years as she matured into the beautiful woman she was destined to become.

51

CHAPTER

Bus Stop Lady

She exploded from the bench at the bus stop. Waving a bottle, she staggered out of the circle of light and into the gathering darkness in pursuit of two preteen girls who were giggling and taunting her. They ran into the distance, laughing. It was over as quickly as it began.

The woman began to sing softly to herself as she tottered back to the end of the bench. She slowly and deliberately poured a circle of booze about her on the sidewalk. People pulled back, giving her plenty of room. They recoiled from the smell of alcohol that permeated the tropical, balmy, Bermuda night air. Her dark ebony skin shone in the streetlight. She looked to be somewhere in her late twenties. Her golden, fake-leopard turban and cape set off her tall, stately features.

Soon the bus came. It lowered itself so riders could get up the steps without difficulty. I filed on and found a seat, glad to be away from the smell of the alcohol. After everyone settled on the bus, she decided to also come on board. She grabbed the handrail, lurched up the steps, swung around, and plopped heavily in the nearest and only empty seat in the front row—right by me. Still muttering to herself, she prepared to settle in. The bus driver, obviously acquainted, spoke soothingly to her. She fidgeted, trying to arrange herself in her seat. She obviously wished to recline, but there wasn't room.

I wish at this point I could report an amazing conversation or some spectacular way in which I was able to reach out and change her life. After all, I was the executive director of a large humanitarian agency. I was traveling in Bermuda to make plans for teaching others from all over North America how to live with compassion. I did this for a living. I constantly studied ways to bring hope to the hopeless.

But it was not to be.

I felt drawn to this woman. What went wrong for her? Why was she in this condition? Did she have children at home? A husband? How many more were just like her—men and women dealing poorly with the harsh realities of life? This was only in the small country of Bermuda. How many more must there be just like her, especially in a country as big as the United States, or even all over the world.

She was just one, and I didn't know what to do. I couldn't help her.

What would Jesus have done? I don't know. What I do know is that I got up and moved. It wasn't one of my finest hours, and I'm not proud of it.

She immediately sprawled out, using the entire row to be comfortable. She seemed glad I was gone. Maybe she wanted to make me uncomfortable so she could have the whole bench. I'll never know. But I do know I moved because she made me nervous.

As I write this many years later, I wonder where she is. What is she doing? Is she sitting under another streetlight somewhere, singing songs, and pouring alcohol about her? She stays on my mind.

Because of her and countless others like her caught in the bondage of addictions, the work of humanitarian agencies will always be needed. Because of her and others like her, there will always be an opportunity to try again. Because of her and others like her, I continue to study ways in which I can move closer not farther away. Because of her and others like her, I stay committed to offering what little help I can.

And I invite you, as you ponder this incident, to join me in renewing your commitment. Resolve again to make a difference somewhere, somehow, in somebody's life. Reach outside of yourself. Get out of your comfort zone. You are wanted—no, not just wanted. You are desperately needed.

I beg you. I implore you. When the chance comes your way, join me in trying to make a difference for someone.

Thank you, lovely lady, whoever you are. Thank you for helping me recognize again my own inadequacies as well as the great need around us. I recognize it is humanly impossible to respond to all the cries; only Jesus can help. Thank you for helping me renew my commitment to God and my neighbor. Thank you for making me uncomfortable.

52

Frantic Mom

It was my birthday. The staff and most of the volunteers were gone for lunch; they all went to the restaurant to celebrate. I prepared to join them, hoping to leave in a few minutes. At that time, one of the few remaining volunteers, an interviewer, appeared in the doorway of my office.

I looked up to find Bella, a sweet, dependable, capable volunteer. I knew she had been interviewing clients all morning, finding out their needs and helping them in whatever way she could. "I'm in the middle of interviewing my last person," she said apologetically, "but I just looked at my watch. It's past one, and I must go. I have another appointment, so I can't stay and finish. Would you be able to take over for me?"

"Of course, no problem." I put down my task at hand and hurried with Bella to meet the client. As we walked briskly through the quiet sorting department and then through the empty food pantry, Bella told me more details about the person she was turning over to me. The woman was traveling through town and had called from a pay phone just as we were closing. She cursed at the person on the phone, demanding they stay open long enough for her to get to us.

Ignoring her obnoxiousness, the receptionist told her to come as quickly as she could.

We stayed open specifically for her, and finally she arrived along with her three children aged five, four, and two. There was no hint of recognition that we had extended our hours just for her; she exuded a loud sense of entitlement. She was rude, demanding, and exceedingly foul-mouthed, Bella told me. This case was going to take more time than Bella had to give today.

Great, I thought. *Not only is this woman making us all late to our appointments, but she's not making it easy to help her.* I opened the door to the small interviewing office, not knowing what to expect.

Bella cordially introduced us. The woman's response to the introduction told me that all Bella had said was true. This woman was exceedingly rude, and her expletives were more than abundant. I asked her some carefully worded questions, hoping to calm her down. She didn't calm down—in fact, things escalated. She claimed to be a member of the Seventh-day Adventist Church, knowing that PACS was supported by that denomination. I didn't believe her because many people claim membership, mistakenly assuming this would give them priority for our services. As her story unfolded, however, I realized her claim to Adventism was true. It wouldn't have mattered because we helped everyone in the same way, trying to discover their needs and alleviate them as best we could.

She loudly demanded help, which I assured her she would get, but she wouldn't listen long enough to let my words penetrate her diatribe. She haughtily informed me they had a place to stay that night, even though the people didn't want them. She and the children would finish their trip the next day. She talked on and on. This interview was not going to be a quickie.

I glanced at the children. They were amazingly well behaved, especially for children so young. They sat quietly, listening, never interrupting, and watching. Their wide eyes were frightened, listless, and almost dull.

On a whim and to change the subject, I asked. "When did your children eat last?"

"They shared a sandwich for supper last night," she said, suddenly uncharacteristically quiet with tears in her voice. Surprised, I looked at my watch. It was almost 2:00 p.m.

I immediately stopped our interview; collected cereal, milk, apples, bread, and peanut butter; and fed the children. They silently ate every bit of it. Mom ate nothing and watched wordlessly.

When the children finished, we talked a little longer. I helped her in every way I could. She was calm, logical, and grateful. As we finished, the kids were getting progressively louder and noisier. They began to run around, chasing each other until she had to tell them to be quiet. Yes, they were boisterous, rambunctious, normal kids. It was a beautiful sight to behold. What a change from their sad, wistful faces just twenty minutes earlier.

Then it hit me. These children were hungry—really hungry. They were so hungry they were no longer functioning as normal children.

I also realized this rude, insulting, vulgar lady was using every trick she knew to fight for the survival of her children. She was desperate, like a cornered animal. Her lashing out was a frantic cry to save her family. As they grew louder, her abrasiveness lessened until it went away completely.

We celebrated my birthday, even though I was late to the party. It didn't really matter anymore. The experience with this mother and her children will be in my memory forever, a birthday present that will impact me for the rest of my life.

It makes me ponder. What about our children? You know—the ones in the grocery store, at church, in the schoolyards, and on the playground. Our children. Do we care about them?

Many children are innocent victims. It's not their fault that Daddy beats up Mommy and they must help her get well. It's not their fault that Mom and Dad did drugs last night and are too wiped out to feed them or change their diapers. It's not their fault when Uncle comes and molests them while they are sleeping in a corner on the floor.

No, it's not their fault, and it's not ours—unless we turn away. What are we doing to help? Are we helping at school, tutoring, or listening to them read? Do we help with the kids at church? How about the neighborhood kids—do we even know their names? Do we know their parents and their struggles?

Take a lesson from this mother. Fight for our children. They are our future. They are God's family. Get involved. Protect them fiercely. Do whatever it takes. They're ours.

53

CHAPTER

Humor or Harassment?

Really? What was this guy thinking? He would not leave me alone. It was lunch hour at PACS, when things typically become quiet and peaceful after the crushing busyness of a full morning. Most of the volunteers leave quite soon after the doors close at noon. A couple of staff were in the back grocery area cleaning and restocking in preparation for the next day. The health clinic was locked until the manager returned from lunch at 1:00 p.m., and the thrift store had no customers while I manned the cash register. A replacement would come to start the afternoon shift.

This guy was insistent. "I'm here to pick up my medicine," he stated. "I tried to get in the clinic, but the door is locked. The only door I can get in is this one for the thrift store."

"I'm sorry," I replied. "They are gone for lunch right now. They'll be back at one o'clock, and I'm sure they'll be happy to help you."

He shifted to his other foot and leaned forward. "But I'm here now. They won't be back for another twenty minutes."

"Yes, I know. Would you like to look around a bit while you're waiting?" I tried to distract him.

"No, I want my medicine. Don't you work here?"

My nametag clearly said, *Executive Director.* "Yes, I work here."

"Then you have keys to the clinic. You can give me my medicine," he reasoned.

"You're right, I do have keys to the clinic. However, your medicine is being held in the pharmacy, and I don't have keys to that room." There was a reason I didn't have that key. No one could legally dispense medicine except a doctor, the nurse, or the clinic manager. I specifically chose not to have access to the pharmacy to protect me from situations exactly like this, though it was the first time I'd ever encountered this scenario.

"That's hogwash," he sputtered. "You're the executive director. You can get into any place you want." He clearly did not believe me.

"Well, that's the one place I cannot get in," I stated. "Please be patient. It won't be long."

"I don't have time to wait around," he stated, moving in close to the cash register. "I want you to get the key and give me my medicine."

"I'm sorry, I can't do that."

"Yes, you can. Now do it!" he demanded, angrily pointing his index finger at me.

"I'd be happy to help you, sir, if I could. I literally don't have a way to get into the pharmacy. It's a beautiful, sunny day outside. Would you like to wait outside if you'd rather not look around in here?"

"I'm not waiting anywhere!" he shouted. "You need to help me. I'm through messing around. I want it now!" He pulled himself up to his full height of well over six feet, towering over my mere five-foot frame.

What was his problem? His prescription was not for an immediate need. He could wait twenty minutes, or even twenty hours, without causing him harm. He puffed himself up into a stance clearly meant to intimidate, his face contorted and angry. I became nervous for my own physical safety and considered pushing the button under the counter for help. When I activated that button, I knew it would send a silent call to the local police station and be fed into the city 911 calling center as an emergency. That step seemed extreme to me, so I thought of an alternative.

I could pick up the phone and state over the intercom in the building, "Would Dr. PACS please come to the thrift store?" That would alert the others in the building that I needed help. But no, when they heard "Dr. PACS," they would know it was code for "call 911," and they would place that call before coming to my aid. That still seemed too extreme, so instead I decided to let him make the choice. "Sir, you need to calm down and wait patiently; otherwise, I'm going to call the police. Would you like me to call the police?" By now it was only fifteen minutes until the clinic would be open for him. I expected him to back down reluctantly and go away.

"Yeah, go ahead and call them," he shot back. "I dare you. You're not going to call the police. You're just too lazy to walk over there and get my medicine."

"I'm sorry you're making me do this. I can't get your medicine, and I can't let you threaten me." I picked up the phone sitting beside the cash register.

Now the guy leaned over the counter, clearly and intentionally getting in my face. I stood tall, feeling very nervous on the inside but looking calm and collected to him—I hoped.

"This is 911, please state your name and address." I gave them the information. "What is the problem?"

"I've got a guy here who wants his medicine, and I can't give it to him. He's becoming belligerent and threatening," I explained to the operator while the guy listened.

"What is he wearing?" the operator asked.

"He's wearing white pants," I began, because that's where my eyes could look without having to confront him. "He's also wearing a green polo shirt." My eyes shifted up and met his. He was staring at me, clearly enjoying my discomfort and forced bravery. I couldn't believe he would stand there and let me turn him in to the police. The operator promised help and kept me on the line until two uniformed police officers sauntered through the thrift store door.

"What's the problem here?" asked one. The guy turned around to face them. "Oh, hi, Eddie," the officer said. "What are you doing? Are you giving this nice lady a hard time?" he asked. The other officer gave Eddie a friendly slap on the back. "Come on outside," he said. "Let's talk."

They took Eddie outside, and while he puffed on a cigarette, the three of them passed the next ten minutes visiting amiably while waiting for the clinic to open. The officers clearly had history with Eddie. They all knew each other well, and he seemed delighted to have their attention.

A few days later, I met Eddie again. This time he stood first in line at a church potluck, still wearing his white pants and green polo shirt.

Eddie scared me. His body language was threatening, and he was a lot bigger than me. I thought he was determined to get his medicine. But as I look back, I remember his curious expression when I called 911. Instead of my actions escalating his anger, he seemed amused, clearly enjoying his interaction with me and anticipating a visit with his friends, the police. As I reminisce, I believe Eddie was simply passing the time he had to wait by harassing me. It was fun for him, like a cat and a mouse, and he knew he meant no harm. I did not know that. He's probably still laughing at the time he frightened that lady in the thrift store.

Was it humor or harassment? Probably neither. Perhaps if I could have focused on him instead of myself, I might had said, "Oh, come on, Eddie. You know I can't do that. Tell me what's up these days while we wait." Perhaps we could have become friends.

54

CHAPTER

Tying a Tie Is a Job Skill

H elen often bubbled with excitement, and today was no exception. She nearly bounced into her appointment in the health clinic. "I'm graduating in a few weeks," she announced proudly. "I've been taking restaurant management at the Western School of Culinary Arts. After graduation I'm going to go on to chef's school." There she stood in the health clinic, proud and happy.

This was wonderful news, and the clinic staff gathered around to congratulate her. The good tidings traveled quickly all over PACS, so I dropped everything and went over to add my congratulations. While we were rejoicing together, Helen told me her story.

"Several years ago, my life fell apart," she began. "My marriage broke up, and suddenly I found myself with no income, no job, and no home."

She described her struggle, finding odd jobs and doing the best she could. She didn't have any specific job skills or work history, so finding work was difficult. She incessantly searched for work but had no luck and soon found herself homeless. She lived out of her car. The stress took its toll, and finally her health gave out.

"I came to this clinic because I have no health insurance or money to pay a doctor. They told me I had diabetes. I had no money for food or a place to live, and now I needed even more money for special food, insulin, and testing strips."

Upon learning her plight, the health clinic staff went into full rescue mode. They connected Helen with special pharmaceutical programs that provided the insulin and testing strips. They took her into the food department and worked with the volunteers there to help her find the right foods to combat her diabetes. They offered nutrition counseling and emotional support. The staff even worked to help Helen find housing. They went above and beyond to help her.

"Everyone was so nice," Helen gushed. "Then I got a chance to go to school. I was so excited, but they required me to wear a special uniform with a spotless white shirt and a burgundy tie."

Slowly, Helen managed to save up enough money to get the required shirt and necktie. She was proud of having acquired the uniform, but she couldn't figure out how to correctly tie her tie.

Again, Helen found help in the health clinic. When she came to her next appointment, she brought her new clothes. She proudly told the doctor she was accepted into the restaurant management program, but she had to wear a shirt and tie as part of the required course uniform. She liked the uniform, but she didn't know how to tie a necktie.

"When the doctor heard that, he stopped everything right in the middle of my doctor's visit and taught me how to tie my tie. Can you believe that?" she bubbled. "After he handed me my prescription, he taught me how to crisscross that thing until I thought I could do it. Then he had me practice over and over; he helped me until I got it right. Then I could go to class.

"I know for sure the doctors and nurses here go the extra mile!" Helen was wearing her shirt and tie for this celebratory appointment. To punctuate her last statement, she said, "Watch me—I can tie it perfectly." She crisscrossed the unwieldy tie like a pro, tying it into a perfect knot under her chin. She didn't even need a mirror.

Helen was right: the doctors and nurses did go the extra mile, and not just for her but for everyone. They exemplified the spirit of PACS while they served the sick and hurting. When God spoke to their hearts, there was no end to their love and compassion. They provided holistic care to the point of teaching skills unrelated to health needs.

But wait—who's to say that teaching job skills is not part of health care?

55

CHAPTER

God Speaks Every Language

A farewell said commonly at PACS was "God bless you." It seemed to be inoffensive to most everyone, and it often brought a joyous response of "God bless you, too." However, it seemed a high percentage of people who came to PACS were not English speaking. It was not unusual to serve people whose language of choice was Russian, Spanish, Vietnamese, Romanian, Korean, Japanese, Lao (Thai), or Cambodian. Sometimes it seemed we were sitting in the heart of the United Nations.

Each nationality had its own preferences in food. The Russians would not eat peanut butter, and they liked tuna packed in oil, not packed in water. One day a Russian gentleman chose to put peanut butter in his cart. It was so unexpected the volunteer helping him queried, "Are you sure you want that?" she asked. "Usually Russian people don't like peanut butter."

"Oh," he replied, "you take a piece of bread, spread some peanut butter on it, and then over that put some jam." His eyes closed, and his face scrunched up in delight. "Mmm!" he exclaimed. That was the turning point, and more and more Russians began to want peanut butter as they became accustomed to an American staple.

The Asians competed over getting bottles of oil, and it seemed every nationality liked rice.

In this hodgepodge of languages, it was difficult to always know how to say, "God bless you." Sometimes it was appropriate to assure people that Jesus loved them, but language could be a major barrier for sharing this kind of comfort. We wanted people to know PACS was a Christian agency, and we would serve their spiritual needs if they were open to that. With that thought in mind, we developed a forest green fabric bookmark with silver lettering that we could send home with the people we served. It read "Jesus Loves Me" in ten different languages. It was received with great delight, and we gave away thousands of them. We hoped this little piece of good news would bring joy wherever it was scattered. It had the PACS address and phone number on it, if anyone wanted to visit the place that freely shared Jesus.

Communicating at a deeper, fundamental level was important to offer more than surface help to those who trusted us enough to open their hearts in respect to their concerns. A question we asked our interviewers to use when people shared their problems was, "Do you have any spiritual resources to help you with this difficulty?" This question gave people the option to say things like, "No, I don't need anything spiritual," or, "Yes, I talk with my priest," or, "Yes, I pray to Buddha every day," or, "No, thank you—I hate God!" This question gave the interviewer an instant understanding of how to approach people in their spiritual comfort zone, and it often opened the door to deep conversations, which could appropriately end with prayer.

It was difficult for some faith-based interviewers to understand the inappropriateness of giving books or other religious material to our clients. Though unintended, giving religious material when it wasn't requested was often perceived by people as a form of manipulation. They felt they must accept the materials and sit through prayer, or else they wouldn't be able to get food or clothing.

This perception was not true because they were never required to participate in anything religious to get what they needed. Free religious materials were provided in book racks if someone wanted them.

Volunteering in an agency like PACS was a learning experience in how to best meet the needs of the people we served without exhibiting silent hopes of some type of reciprocal behavior in return for help. We called this disinterested benevolence, which simply meant helping with no expectations. Another way we checked our motives was to honestly ask ourselves, "What's in this for the client? What's in this for us?"

If a person asked for spiritual or religious information, we were happy to supply that, but even offering to pray with them was done very carefully to make sure people did not feel coerced, belittled, or offended. We asked, "May I pray *with* you?" rather than, "May I pray *for* you?" That was a crucial difference in the minds of our clients.

Volunteers were the driving force of the agency. We absolutely depended on volunteers, and it was always a happy day when someone wanted to volunteer. One day someone came asking to volunteer, but just for the day. She was not planning to stay, so she declined giving me any information about herself, even her name. Normally I would not allow someone to volunteer who refused to sign up properly because it put our insurance at risk, but she only wanted to stay one day, so I relented and assigned her to a job handing out clothes. She settled in, doing well.

During the morning, a couple came in for help who were new to PACS. The interviewer worked hard to communicate with them. They seemed to have a specific need, but we could not figure out what it was. Both were deaf and unable to speak, making communication very difficult. Even writing notes did not work.

Word spread throughout the agency to see whether anyone could communicate with this couple. It wasn't long before the new volunteer discovered the problem. "Let me help," she said eagerly. "Where are they?"

We led her from where she was handing out clothes to the interview room to meet the couple. She immediately began to talk to the couple in sign language. Their faces broke into relieved smiles, and they were able to get what they needed. She even gave them one of the forest green fabric bookmarks with "Jesus Loves Me" in American Sign Language printed at the bottom.

Who was this volunteer? Where did she come from? Was she an angel?

"No, I'm not an angel," she said. "I grew up with two deaf parents, and we used sign language in our home." Consequently, she had developed fluent sign language skills as a child.

We begged her to come regularly, but she never returned, and neither did the couple who needed her specialized help.

56

CHAPTER

TP for the Needy

Remember when traveling around the world meant a whole new experience in acceptable materials for personal hygiene?

Yes, it seems that whatever country one visited, even different places within a country, a person could find an array of colors, styles, and textures of that very necessary item: toilet paper, or TP. On my first trip abroad, I was so intrigued by the various types of TP that I collected samples and made a scrapbook of them.

Although I'm sure there are some countries where TP is still textured, colorful, or unusual, it seems that at least in Europe, things are getting more standardized, with soft and gentle becoming the boring norm. All in all, no matter what the feel or how absorbent, I'm sure you'll agree TP is a most important commodity.

There must be higher, loftier subjects than TP for a book like this, but as routine, mundane, and even disgusting as it may be, we discovered at PACS that the Lord thinks TP is mighty important.

For those caught in, or anticipating, disastrous conditions such as fires, floods, hurricanes, or tornadoes, it is always important to have TP in a disaster kit so it can be grabbed and taken with you at a moment's notice. This is common knowledge for home disaster preparation.

But there are other situations not so commonly thought of that also can leave a person without the necessary materials to tend to personal hygiene. At PACS, we discovered that for many people, TP is a luxury. When a person's life is suddenly uprooted, such as in domestic violence or eviction, TP is not something a person usually thinks to grab on the way out the door. When money must be divided between food and medicines, TP often becomes a luxury. Homeless people struggle to find TP on a consistent basis, making a simple thing like tending to personal hygiene a constant and time-consuming quest.

One day a mother came, requesting toilet paper from PACS in addition to food. We tried to keep a small supply stashed away for requests like hers. We didn't always have any, but today she was in luck. When I gave her the toilet paper, I asked, "What do you do when you can't afford any toilet paper, and you can't get any from PACS?"

"We have to use socks," she replied matter-of-factly.

Socks? Really? This was America. How could it be that this mother was forced to tell her children to use socks for toilet paper when the money was tight? I was shocked by this revelation and relayed it to the other staff and volunteers.

We resolved to have a TP drive, so we began advertising. It seemed a little strange to advertise for toilet paper, with some people concerned about the sensitivity of the topic. We requested donations of partial rolls because most of the time those were easiest to handle, especially for the homeless and people caught in transition. Among ourselves we referred to these partial rolls as "used toilet paper." We advertised to churches, schools, and people all over the city, hoping to find some people who would bring us some rolls over the next few weeks.

We were not inundated with a huge amount of calls donating partial rolls of toilet paper. We got a few rolls from scattered churches and isolated individuals, which was helpful. Then one day I got a call from someone saying, "You still need toilet paper?"

"Yes, absolutely," I replied.

"Good," the caller responded. "I've got several cases you can have!"

Wow, this was more like what we needed. We were excited and arranged to get them as quickly as we could.

Then, another phone call came. "Did I see that you need toilet paper?"

"Yes, we do," I responded.

"If you can come and get them," the caller told me, "I can give you a couple pallets of partial rolls!" We immediately dispatched our truck driver to go pick the pallets up, and we suddenly had more TP than we had ever imagined.

When I asked where the donor got cases of partial toilet paper rolls, his answer was simply, "I've got my sources."

Whatever his sources, the Lord provided TP, and we didn't have to turn away anyone for a very long time.

Do you remember the passage in Matthew 6:25 (KJV), where it says, "Therefore I tell you, do not worry about your life, what you will eat or drink; or about your body, what you will wear. Is not life more than food, and the body more than clothes"? If you read verses 25–34, it plainly says that the Lord cares for His children and will supply their needs. If He cares about TP, I know He cares about your needs. Nothing is insignificant to Him. Trust His promises; He never fails.

57

CHAPTER ═══════════════════════════════

Cancer Free

H er voice was exuberant. Even over the phone, it was easy to tell
how elated she was.

"Guess what? Guess what? After sixteen months, I'm cancer
free!"

Karen's mind flashed back to that visit so very long ago when
Cindy came in to see a doctor. As Cindy prepared to leave after her
doctor's visit that day, Karen, the health clinic manager, playfully
said, "So, when was the last time you had your annual exam?"

"Oh, I haven't had one for years," Cindy replied lightly. "Maybe,
sometime, I'll do that," she added dismissively.

"Well, what about right now?" asked Karen, now serious. "The
patient coming after you is our last appointment. She just cancelled,
so the doctor has time. It's quitting time, so no one else is coming.
It won't take long, and we'll stay here until you're done." Cindy was
not really interested, but she didn't flatly refuse, so Karen pressed
her. "Really, why don't you just do it while you're here? That way you
don't have to make another appointment and find a way to come in."

For many years, the health clinic partnered with a cancer-
detection program offered to women who had no money to see a

doctor. This program offered free breast exams, mammograms, and all other treatments, including chemo, radiation, and surgery if the testing revealed anything abnormal. This was a major help for women, especially those who might suspect something but refrained from getting medical attention because they could not afford the expense. However, the opportunity for free exams was not well-known, so Karen explained it in detail to Cindy. Finally, with a bit of persuasion, Cindy reluctantly consented to have the exam. At least it wouldn't cost her anything, and she wouldn't have to worry about doing it later. After all, there was an empty appointment slot, and she could get the exam over with. *Then Karen won't keep asking about it every time I come to see the doctor,* Cindy reasoned to herself.

The volunteer nurse helped Cindy prepare for the exam, and then the doctor quickly but thoroughly went through the routine of physically checking to rule out any abnormalities. It didn't take too long before the doctor finished, had a short consultation with Cindy, and came back to the doctor's desk to make notes.

Cindy emerged from the exam room slowly and soberly. The doctor had detected a suspicious lump in her breast. Now she needed another appointment for a mammogram. The results of the mammogram led to another appointment to have a biopsy. The biopsy confirmed the lump was malignant, which led to more appointments for surgery, followed by many more appointments for grueling rounds of chemotherapy and radiation. Cindy's life was turned upside down and seemed to revolve around appointments, appointments, and more appointments. The weeks turned into months as treatments and X-rays of various types filled her days. Finally, the rounds of treatments and doctors were over; she was told to come back after a few months for routine checking to make sure the cancer was gone.

Sixteen months later, she called us with her good news. She was cancer free!

I sometimes wonder, *What if the doctor had decided to go home early that day because the last patient had cancelled? What if the*

volunteer nurses hadn't been willing to put in a few extra minutes?
What if no one had encouraged Cindy to stay for an exam?

But what-ifs don't really matter. What's important is that Karen
and the crew did urge Cindy to get her exam, the doctor did stay, and
the nurses did help. Together, they went beyond what was expected.
They cared about Cindy and her future. That's one thing about the
health clinic: every one of the people volunteering there went the
extra mile in compassionate caring not just on that day but on every
day. They truly loved their work and those they selflessly served.
They lived out the principles embodied in their beliefs in Jesus and
His caring ministry while He was here on Earth. The Lord blessed
them, and the Lord blessed their dearly beloved patients.

58

CHAPTER

The Clash of Hidden Rules

"I *need* this coat!" she screamed at me. The impact of her hot breath in my face, menacing stance, angry face, and clenched fist made me want to recoil in submission. But I couldn't. I had to stand my ground. This was an important showdown, one I had to meet head-on—or so I thought.

Earlier that morning, the woman had come to PACS to get a coat for her six-year-old daughter. It was October, and the nights were frosty, followed by chilly and often wet days. Her daughter needed something warm to wear to school. The woman was making a legitimate request that we wanted to honor.

The person who'd requested my help with this matter had disappeared; it was just me and the lady standing in the middle of the coat aisle and screaming at me. The thrift store was bustling with other customers choosing clothes and looking at shoes and other items. Suddenly, I realized the store was no longer humming with the noise of shopping. All customers had stopped their purchasing. As one, they turned to gaze upon the scene unfolding in the coat department.

I quietly reiterated, "I'm sorry, this coat is too big for your daughter. It is large enough to fit you." I noted silently she was wearing a nice coat capable of keeping her very warm. She did not need another coat.

The woman clutched the full-length, faux leopard, fuzzy fur coat to her bosom. "I'll let her wear it," she screamed. "We will share this coat. I *need* this coat!" Her voice rose in volume with each sentence. By then she was screaming at the top of her voice. With every increasing decibel, she punctuated her points with flaming obscenities and vicious name-calling meant to intimidate me. She used words I had never heard before, but I had no doubt as to their meaning.

I tried to quietly and calmly reason with her and help her see that her daughter needed to be warm, that the coat would drag on the ground and get terribly dirty, and many other things that I thought might help her change her mind. I told her I'd be more than happy to let her have another coat that would fit her daughter. But my words only fueled her fury until her rage was palpable. The people in the store were frozen in suspense. What would happen?

Without warning, the woman threw down the coat and stomped down the aisle toward the front door. Throwing angry obscenities over her shoulder, she finally disappeared without a coat for her daughter. Silence reigned for a few seconds. Shoppers absorbed the sudden quietness. Sad for her daughter, I picked up the coat, hung it up, and turned to go back to my office. On my way down the aisle, several shoppers approached me, apologizing for the episode. They thoughtfully offered me consolation in a difficult and embarrassing situation.

This incident still haunts me. What was happening under the surface? What cues had I missed? What was it in this situation that I didn't understand? There must have been an underlying cause for the extreme rage and anger spewing from this otherwise attractive and engaging woman.

Over the years, I've learned a few things. One thing I've learned is there are unwritten, hidden rules that govern each of us. They are things we've learned without knowing it from the way we've been brought up; from our families, our relatives, our friends, school, and church; and from wherever we find ourselves economically in society.

Some people identify economic differences in society as class differences. They differentiate between lower, middle, and upper classes in America. These differences are based solely on wealth. There are hidden rules in each of these classes that dictate our values and responses to life situations.[1] Most of us don't realize this. The mistaken expectation of most middle-class Americans is, "If you look like me and you talk like me, then you also think like me." Of course, I'm making broad generalizations applied to class differences. It is important to remember that not everyone fits the mold.

In my middle-class upbringing, I realized that I operated from certain expectations, which gave me expectations of having a certain future; I could effect change by making certain decisions, and that I had a place in the context of my country. I've now learned that my understanding is distinctly different from those who are wealthy.

Wealthy people often don't worry about the future in the same way I do—it's already assured for them. They don't worry about producing change as much as keeping things stable. Many wealthy people don't concern themselves with where they fit in their country; their view is much more global, with a concern of how they fit into the world.

On the other hand, people from impoverished classes—especially those who find themselves in generational poverty, where being poor has been the norm for their family—have a different

---

[1] There is much to be read on this subject. This book is not intended to provide scholarly resources, but I urge you to explore the writings of Ruby Payne and Donna Beegle for more in-depth information. Other resources can be found by searching for materials on "hidden class rules."

view of how to respond to life. People who find themselves in generational poverty may know, without a doubt, that there is no other way of life for them. They will always be poor, they will never effect change in their neighborhoods or their family situations, their decisions are of no value, the future is now, and their place is in their own neighborhood because many rarely travel beyond a few square miles from home.

Here's an example of how our hidden values effect our decisions. Remember, these are broad generalities. (1) A wealthy person needs a job so she speaks to someone who gets her one, or she lives on family wealth. (2) A middle-class person needs a job, so he sends out resumes everywhere, knowing he may have to move away, leaving friends and family to find work. (3) A lower-class person needs a job, so she lets her friends know, and maybe she sends out a few local resumes in hopes of finding something; moving is not considered.

Here's an example of value differences. Again, remember there are many variations of these generalities. (1) Wealthy classes often tend to aspire for one-of-a-kind things, a legacy, a degree, or status; a global outlook is the norm. 2) Middle-class people often aspire to achieve and be successful, to own things (such as a fancy car, the latest gadgets, or clothes); families and relationships may have to be put aside in pursuit of other things, and an education is important in creating the means to afford things. (3) Lower classes value family and relationships above all, and entertainment is very important; education is not viewed as helpful in obtaining those values.

These hidden values often create conflicts when we try to help people. Take for example the times when well-meaning people, organizations, and church groups join around the holidays to create food baskets or get Christmas presents for families who are struggling. How many times have you heard, "I knocked on their door to deliver the gifts and food, and when they opened it, there was a big-screen TV. I can't even afford one of those. Why don't they use that money for food?"

This is when hidden rules show themselves. The ones with the big-screen TV are living according to the hidden rules of their class. That TV makes their home the center of fellowship for all their friends and family while providing entertainment. That TV brings them love and acceptance from those most important to them. From their viewpoint, it is certain that they will always be poor, and no amount of saving will change that fact. When they get a little money, it is logical that it be used for the values that are most important: families, relationship, and entertainment. Live for now, because a there is no hope of anything different in the future. And we in turn think exactly like middle-class Americans because we are certain that saving our money will make life better in the long run.

Why are these things important? Why was the situation I encountered so volatile? I believe it was a clash in our value differences. I was using all my middle-class logic to make my case. This woman saw a coat that would bring her the admiration of her friends and family. She would be praised and adulated for her prize. It would bring her love and acceptance. In her world, these values were worth making a huge scene in hopes of being successful.

And I ponder now, *How should I have responded? What could I have done differently to honor her values? What would Jesus have done? If someone has a different lens than mine regarding how they understand the world, are they wrong? Are hidden values moral?* I'm not sure of all the answers, but I do know my deeper understanding of hidden values gives me the freedom to more openly view the puzzling decisions of others who live different from me.

59

CHAPTER ════════════════════

Meeting the Devil

"Have you met the devil yet?" he asked pointedly.

"What?" came my puzzled reply. I heard his question, but I didn't fully grasp why he was asking or the context of how to answer. I needed a little more time to absorb the full import of his words without answering glibly.

We were both far from home, somewhere in the United States at a national Adventist Community Services convention, where I had just finished presenting stories and experiences of PACS, telling of God's leading in our agency. As usual, I talked about times of amazing and providential care, told of God's leading in our decision making, and gave Him the glory, hoping to inspire others to increased faith and reliance on God as they served in their own community service agencies. When I finished the talk, people came forward to chat and ask questions.

"Have you met the devil?" he repeated, stating it a little louder and more as a demand. "Because if you haven't met the devil, then what you're doing at PACS is not enough to worry him. It may seem like good things are happening, but none of it matters if the devil doesn't care. Satan always shows up when God is winning."

This was not a new concept to me. In fact, I'd been tempted to think that way myself at times. I don't remember my answer, but his question stays with me and causes me to reflect on the seemingly crush of busyness, sometimes bordering on craziness, that seemed to be normal at PACS.

Every morning we had worship with the staff and volunteers. We finished with prayer and then announcements. After announcements and a brief time of cheery chitchat, everyone went to their respective places throughout the building to be ready for the day. The intake manager went to the far end of the building and opened the front door at precisely 9:00 a.m. to welcome the line of people waiting for food, clothing, and health care. The line, sometimes as many as fifty people, formed under an awning and would often curl around the building and into the parking lot.

This time in the morning was usually peaceful, but not always. Forming a line did not always fit with the cultural practices of some of the people. They did not want to wait. When they came in the door, they were expected to take a number, just like they had to do in other places such as the social security office and department of motor vehicles. The intake manager soon learned to hand out the numbers herself, one by one, so people wouldn't take multiple numbers for their friends who had not yet arrived.

Some cultures and economic classes settle conflict physically. Other classes and cultures use forceful persuasion, often arguing loudly, but they don't throw punches or shove as quickly. The third way of settling differences is through negotiation. It was not unusual for all these tactics to show themselves while people were waiting in line, making it necessary for the intake manager to be masterful in her handling of the various situations that could quickly erupt.

In Hebrews 1:14, the Bible says each person who loves God is given angels to be with them and protect them. The Bible also mentions evil angels in many places, especially in Matthew, Mark, Luke, and John, when recounting the earthly ministry of Jesus. I believe people have good or evil angels that accompany them depending on the trajectory and circumstances of their lives and the choices they make.

At times, it seemed that when the front door was opened, with people jostling and pushing to be first, evil angels also entered, and an atmosphere invaded the agency, shattering the peace found in morning worship. People were easily irritated, pushed, shoved, called each other names, and occasionally threw punches. Volunteers would have to respond, making a warm welcome hard to maintain. Sometimes that negative atmosphere would pervade the entire agency. Patience was in short supply as people would argue, complain, and demand. One morning, my intake manager came to me and asked, "Can we pray together? I feel a presence in this building that needs to be rebuked."

We prayed for the presence of God's holy angels so that they would dispel the spirit of oppression and chaos infecting the agency. The rest of the morning went very smoothly. This became a practice for us whenever we sensed a spirit of anger and antagonism hovering over our work.

Another time, Veronica, an intake interviewer, burst into my office and shut the door behind her. Normally a calm, quiet-spoken person, she announced, "I just saw Satan!"

"Oh? Tell me about it," I responded, coming out from behind my desk while inviting her to sit with me at the small round table allowing for more intimate conversation. She was a serious, God-fearing woman, so I knew she was not making this up.

"Well," she said, looking down at her clenched hands, "I was interviewing this person, and we were talking about the situation. I wrote down a few notes on the card in front of me, and when I looked up, instead the person sitting there, the devil was looking back at me."

"What did you do?" I asked curiously.

"I sent a quick prayer to heaven, and immediately the devil went away. Then all I saw was the person I had been interviewing. Can we pray together?"

We prayed together, asking for a legion of angels and specific protection for Veronica. We also prayed that the Lord would banish this evil from our midst that morning.

His question remains: "Have you seen the devil?" I'm not convinced it's a good success indicator, but the answer is, "Yes, without a doubt."

60

CHAPTER

Mike's Ring

M ike was devastated. His most prized possession was gone. The expensive ring meant a lot to him. He smiled as he remembered that most amazing Father's Day when he'd received the exquisitely boxed ring while surrounded by his four children. He was proud of them. They were older and grown up, and he knew their affection was wrapped in their gift, an expensive gem snuggled in a setting chosen just for him. It was valuable and dear to his heart.

Now it was missing.

He first missed it while he was working one Friday in the thrift store. Mike searched high and low. When he couldn't find the ring, Mike enlisted the help of the other workers, and finally everyone was looking for Mike's ring.

The other workers searched everywhere, even places where Mike was sure he had not been. They prayed silently and then gathered in groups to pray about the ring. They fully expected to find it, but where?

Finally, the clock showed it was time to close the store for the weekend. The ring was still missing. Even though Mike was sure he'd lost the ring at the store, with some hopefulness, he went home to search for the elusive treasure. *Maybe I didn't wear it today,* he thought to himself. At home, he looked under furniture, between the couch cushions, and across all the floors. It wasn't anywhere.

The weekend passed with Mike becoming more and more despondent. He did not tell his children about his despair, hoping somehow the ring would appear. The next Monday found Mike again helping customers with their transactions. Just as on the previous Friday, he rang up purchases at the cash register, bagged the items, and helped carry the customer's packages out to their cars. Though he smiled and visited cheerfully with customers and fellow workers, on the inside his heart was heavy.

The morning hours dragged on, with Mike glancing frequently at the clock. How would he ever tell his children that his precious ring was gone? The knot in his stomach tightened. He hadn't had much experience with prayer, and he wondered how concerned God would be for his loss, even though it felt monumental to Mike. After all, it was just a small ring. Feeling tired and deflated, Mike left for lunch.

Upon returning from lunch, Mike again took up his position at the cash register. Meeting and greeting the customers helped distract him from his loss.

Early in the afternoon, a customer approached the cash register. She didn't have any items to buy, so Mike asked if she needed help. "Yes," she answered. "I was just wondering, did you lose a ring?"

"Why yes, yes I did!" Mike replied, eagerly hoping for good news.

The lady told him her story. "I came in last Friday and purchased some things from you. You put them in bags for me and helped me carry them to the car. I was so grateful because I had my handicapped son with me, and it's hard to manage packages and push his wheelchair. You were amazing with him, talking to him and teaching him how to do high-fives even though it was a struggle for him. He loves coming here because you are always so friendly to him.

"When I got home and unpacked my things, there was a gorgeous ring in the bottom of one of the bags. I figured it must be yours. My husband didn't want me to return the ring because he thought it was probably expensive, but I insisted. You were so nice to my son; I could not keep your valuable ring." She cried. "What's more, it was the first time ever that my son actually turned his hand over by himself, which he did when he returned your high-fives."

Mike said later, "I'm sure now that God does care about the little things. My faith is stronger, and I'm amazed. God not only returned my ring but also brought healing to someone else through this experience. Wow, just wow!"

61

CHAPTER ================================

The Bible Is a Bestseller

There's a reason the Bible is still a bestseller. Many people treasure it and hold it dear to their hearts. It brings them joy, hope, comfort, and instruction. This is true all over the world, and it was also true in the city of Portland, Oregon. For some reason, I surmised that the Bible was not as important to many of the people who came to PACS. I was wrong.

When we offered a Bible to people, especially the homeless, they would gladly take it. Many had a surprising amount of knowledge about the stories in the Bible, and most could refer to a passage they found especially comforting. Sometimes their memories were a little sketchy about the exact details, but they still had feelings of warmth about having a Bible in their hands.

The conundrum around Bibles was that a lot of people who donated to PACS had a couple, or even several, Bibles on their bookshelves. It was common to donate clothes, furniture, food, or money to PACS, but people didn't think about donating Bibles. Bibles were a very precious commodity. We never had enough, so sometimes we would put out a plea to the community and churches to look through their bookshelves and pull out any extra Bibles they weren't using. This would prompt people's memory and would usually result in generous donations of used Bibles.

At PACS, Bibles were always free; we placed them right by the cash register. The first time we put them out for people to take, I was surprised at how quickly they disappeared. Once, a man gratefully accepted a Bible, went outside the front glass door, and sat on the curb in front of the large, floor-to-ceiling windows in the warm sun. He thumbed back and forth through the pages for a long time, crying over the joy of having such a blessed book all his own.

On one occasion, after we advertised a community Bible roundup hoping people would donate their extra Bibles, someone gave us a check to go buy new Bibles. This sent us on a quest to find the best prices, and it gave us a chance to fill a frequent request for Romanian Bibles. We were excited and ordered a large quantity of Bibles in English, Romanian, and other languages.

Finally, the long-anticipated Bibles arrived. We put them out a few at a time, hoping to make them last longer. We gave out a couple Romanian Bibles, and word began to spread, "PACS has Bibles in Romanian. Go ask for one." People came to specifically ask for Bibles in Romanian.

"Do you have Romanian Bibles left?" asked one man in a heavy accent. His English was limited, but he knew how to ask for a Bible.

"Yes," replied the thrift shop manager. "Let me get you one." She went into the small storage room where the box of Bibles was kept and found one for him. "Here you go," she said, holding it out to him.

The man grabbed the Bible and clutched it to his chest dramatically. "Oh, thank you, thank you," he exclaimed. He reached out to her and engulfed her in a big hug while kissing her enthusiastically on both cheeks. "Thank you, thank you," he repeated over and over.

Then he raised the Bible over his head and went running up one aisle and down another, "Thank you, thank you, thank you!" he shouted exuberantly as he ran. He ran all around the thrift store, through the quilt and linen section, through the coats, around the pants, though the children's clothes, by the shoes, and under the pictures on the back wall. "Thank you, thank you, thank you!" he gushed repeatedly. He didn't have the English words to express his gratitude more graphically.

Upon returning to the cash register, he enveloped the manager in another huge bear hug, again placing kisses on both of her cheeks. "Thank you, thank you," he continued as he raised his Bible over his head again and ran out the door into the parking lot. The manager heard him shouting, "Thank you, thank you," until she couldn't hear him any longer and the door closed behind him.

All over the world, the Bible is a bestseller, but not at PACS. Bibles were popular, but they were not bestsellers simply because they were priceless. God's grace is always free, and so were the Bibles to anyone who would accept one.

62

CHAPTER ══════════════════════════

Keeping Food Out
of the Landfill

Each morning, drivers from PACS would make the rounds to various grocery stores in the Portland area. We routinely picked up food donations from stores such as Trader Joe's, Safeway, Oroweat, and Thriftway. We owned a small cube van with a lift gate that had been used for this job for several years, provided by a miracle of God.

Every year, more and more people seemed to need food. As we prayed for resources to meet the rapidly increasing need for food, our suppliers became even more generous. Gradually it became obvious our truck was too small to handle the increase. We couldn't get to all the stores in a day without overloading the truck. It was crucial to not miss a day, or else stores would change their loyalties and start giving the food to whatever agency could be there without fail every morning when they opened. There was a lot of competition for food among the agencies, so losing an account because we didn't have the equipment to haul it properly would be devastating. The volunteers gallantly tried to keep up with the increasing demand to meet every appointment every morning. Consequently, we began handling too much in each load, straining the truck beyond its capacity. Twice the lift gate broke and crashed to the ground. Fortunately, no one was hurt. We badly needed an additional, bigger truck so we could safely make our rounds.

Faced with this dilemma, we decided to submit a grant request to Metro Recycling, which we called Metro, to fund a new truck for $35,000. It would be a twenty-foot truck just under the commercial rating, so volunteers could drive it without a commercial license and we wouldn't be assessed the extra expense of Department of Motor Vehicle fees.

Metro was very gracious and assured me they would seriously consider our request. They told me I must show them how much food we would divert from becoming landfill by our increased ability to salvage it from stores that would otherwise dump it. They wanted to help feed the hungry, but that was not the reason Metro existed. They needed to show that their charity was an extension of their mission, which was to promote recycling and keep garbage out of the local dumps. Usually companies focused on how much they helped the poor by the amount of money or equipment they gave to feed the hungry, so Metro's requirements necessitated a very different way of writing a request.

The grantwriter wrote carefully, wordsmithing over and over until she finally had it right. Someone at Metro coached us because she liked our proposal and wanted to fund it. Finally, we made the required amount of copies, bound and signed by our governing board chairman according to the proposal directions. We submitted the request and waited expectantly.

After about four months, the eagerly anticipated letter arrived. We gathered around, expecting to receive a check and certain that our new truck was finally funded. We had already started thanking God for the truck. When I opened it, I read, "We regret to inform you that we cannot approve your request for a new truck." Suddenly our thanks turned into questioning. What had gone wrong?

I was shocked and couldn't understand it. We needed that truck, and it seemed that God had directed us to Metro. Metro had even told us how to write the grant request. After a couple days of processing my disappointment, I phoned the Metro contact for an explanation.

"Oh, that," she said. "Our granting committee reviewed your request and felt it was not complete. You gave us good information, but the committee decided your agency needs a refrigerated truck, so they denied your petition. They suggested you rewrite your grant, asking for $120,000 to cover a truck with heavier suspension and refrigeration, which they will then review."

We went back to the drawing board, got new quotes, and refigured our needs. We rewrote the proposal for $120,000 and sent it in, and Metro awarded us $75,000. They wanted us to approach additional funders to help support the cost of the complete proposal.

With the metro grant in hand, we submitted the same request to two other funders, and the full $120,000 was donated. Not only did we receive the $75,000 for the truck, but the additional $45,000 covered the fuel and maintenance for three years. This was much more than we'd originally thought we needed.

As it turned out, a refrigerated truck was exactly what we needed all along, but we didn't know it. We had been aiming too low. The Lord knew our need before we did.

The Lord knew the Oregon Food Bank was working on forming an agreement with Albertson's grocery store chain to donate food to agencies like ours. He knew that in six months, Albertson's would team up with the Oregon Food Bank but would stipulate that whoever picked up the food must have a refrigerated truck. Our agency was the only agency in the whole Portland metropolitan area that met this requirement. The Lord blessed us with more than we could ever have dreamed, both in safe and adequate equipment and in providing more food for the hungry.

63

CHAPTER

Heating Oil

I walked by the empty desk. The phone rang loudly, incessantly, and demandingly. Where was everyone? We never had enough help, it seemed. The receptionist who should have been answering the phone was nowhere in sight. This was not unusual at PACS because many visitors came and wanted to see what we did and how we ran our organization. We often had to give impromptu tours or escort them to someone else who could show them around. Other times, people came who wanted to become volunteers or simply had questions. This was a normal, happy part of life at PACS, and we were pleased to oblige.

But today was different. It was almost quitting time, and I had important things demanding my attention that had to be done before I could leave. I was not hired to be the receptionist. Overworked, tired, and impatient, I heaved a sigh of resignation, turned back, reached over the desk, and reluctantly picked up the phone.

Fortunately, it was a routine call—or so I thought. A woman wanted to give an in-kind donation to PACS; in other words, she wanted to give something other than money, like clothes, furniture, food, or maybe even a car. I told her when she brought it in, we would be happy to provide a receipt, and I prepared to hang up. But the donor was not ready to hang up. She wanted to talk about what she planned to give us. This was not unusual either because people were often excited about their gifts and wanted to tell us about how important something was to them. I prepared to listen, acting patient but feeling stressed.

The caller explained she wanted to donate thirty gallons of heating oil, so she could not bring it to us. Surprised, I knew this unusual donation was beyond our ability to handle, so I did what I had never done before. I tactfully declined the gift and thanked her for thinking about PACS. She was genuinely disappointed because she was sure there must be someone who could use the heating oil. She pressed me to figure out a way to accept it. I tried to make her feel better by asking for her name and phone number in case I heard of someone who might need the oil. I kept the phone to my ear while I moved carefully around the desk to sit in the empty receptionist chair. I searched for a pen and paper to take her contact information. I was polite and dutifully wrote it all down even though no one had ever donated or asked for heating oil in all the years I'd worked at PACS. I'd pretty much seen it all and knew I would never talk with her again. We both hung up. She was happy that maybe someone would want her oil, and I was relieved to be able to get back to my own work.

I rose from the chair and turned wearily toward my office when the phone rang again. I was already detained, so I resignedly sat back down and answered it.

"Portland Adventist Community Services, can I help you?" It was a long, wordy way to answer the phone, but I had mastered it well.

"Do you give money?" a man asked abruptly.

"No, I'm sorry, we don't. There are other agencies that sometimes have money. Would you like their phone numbers?" I responded. A rule we always tried to teach our clients was, "If someone tells you they can't help you, never hang up the phone until you have another number to call. Never leave a call with no options left." Because I couldn't help him myself, I offered this man other phone numbers where he might possibly find what he needed.

Instead of taking the numbers I offered him, the caller rushed on. "I have a wife and two small children. One child is two years old, and the other is just seven months." My heart sank. "I have a job now," he continued proudly, "and we just moved into a tiny little house. We paid the rent, but we have no heat. I need money to pay for heat." I felt bad. This was a dire predicament, especially because it was January and the weather had been unusually cold, but I didn't have any money. I was proud that he had a job and was providing for his family, and I was concerned about them because I knew the babies could not survive this harsh winter weather with no heat.

After talking with him a little while, I asked him if the heat in the house was gas or electricity. "Neither," he replied. "It's oil."

Oil? Oil! I couldn't believe my ears. Calm on the outside but with bated breath, I queried, "How much oil do you need?" Getting excited, I searched frantically for the piece of paper with the lady's name and phone number who wanted to give thirty gallons of heating oil.

He answered, "The tank holds thirty gallons." Filled with wonder and awe, I discovered the piece of paper still in my hand; I hadn't even had a chance to put it down. I told him someone had just called hoping to give away thirty gallons of oil. He quickly found a pencil and paper, so relieved and elated that he could hardly write down the information. I learned later that he called the woman immediately, and they were able to arrange for the delivery.

Was it fate, chance, luck, serendipity, or a miracle? I went back to my office, collapsed in my chair, put my head in my hands, and marveled how the Lord had worked out His purposes. All He needed was a middleman, and that was me. He knew I didn't need physical rest like I thought I did. In fact, He put me to work. He had much more important work for me to do than I'd been planning to get done on my own. I hadn't rested, but I was completely rejuvenated, thanking Him over and over for His never-failing creativity in meeting the needs of His children, the need of the donor, the need of the family, and even my need. I was grateful and humbled that He used me even in my grumpy frame of mind, of which I repented immediately. I realized again what God means when He says, "For My yoke is easy, and my burden is light" (Matthew 11:30 NKJV).

CONCLUSION

Though these stories occurred at PACS, they do not belong to PACS alone; they will be familiar examples of life to anyone who has been or decides to become involved in this type of Christlike service.

Every day, people wrestle with poverty, hunger, and degradation. Every day, new individuals and families plummet into hard times. Every day, legions of angels work beside faithful volunteers, pastors, teachers, social workers, and ordinary people like you and me to bring relief where possible. We hurt when those around us hurt. Yes, we care—all of us care—and we must never quit caring.

Let your faith rest in these stories. Remember these miracles when life seems bleak. The same God who alternately cried, caressed, blessed, and rejoiced over His children in these stories lives today. He will cry, caress, bless, and rejoice over you just as He did over His children in Bible times, just as He did through the ages, and just as He did (and still does) at PACS. He longs to be your shield and fortress, an ever-present help in time of trouble. Ask Him. Trust Him. Believe Him.

I hope these stories inspired and encouraged you to find a renewed love for your neighbors. I hope they helped to remove the fear of walking with those who make us feel uncomfortable. This is where raw Christianity becomes the norm. As Walt Blehm (his real name), one of PACS' governing board chairmen, once said, "PACS is a lab for religion." Each of us is called to participate in this laboratory in some way. Do you feel Him tugging your heart to be part of His cadre of hard-living people?

A FINAL THOUGHT

If you wish to help the work of PACS, you may reach them at:

www.**pacsonline.org**

Or by calling:

503-252-8500

Portland Adventist Community Services
11020 NE Halsey St.
Portland, Oregon 97220